NEWMAN FOR EVERYONE

By the same author:

An Augustine Treasury, Boston, 1981.

A Philosopher's Search for the Infinite,
New York, 1983.

An Aquinas Treasury, Arlington, 1988.

*Inferring God's Existence: Anselm, Aquinas
and Kant*, Kansas City, 1993.

Newman for Everyone

101 Questions answered
imaginatively by Newman

Edited by

JULES M. BRADY, SJ

Professor of Philosophy
Rockhurst College

ALBA · HOUSE   alba house   NEW · YORK

SOCIETY OF ST. PAUL, 2187 VICTORY BLVD., STATEN ISLAND, NEW YORK 10314

ST PAULS

Library of Congress Cataloging-in-Publication Data

Newman, John Henry, 1801-1890.
   Newman for everyone : 101 questions answered imaginatively by
Newman / edited by Jules M. Brady.
      p.   cm.
   Includes bibliographical references.
   ISBN 0-8189-0736-3
   1. Catholic Church — Doctrines — Miscellanea.   I. Brady, Jules M.
II. Title.
BX1754.3.N48   1996
230'.2 — dc20   96-1267
                                    CIP

Imprimi Potest:
E. Edward Kinerk, SJ
Censor Librorum

Produced and designed in the United States of America by the
Fathers and Brothers of the Society of St. Paul,
2187 Victory Boulevard, Staten Island, New York 10314,
as part of their communications apostolate.

ISBN: 0-8189-0736-3

Printing Information:

Current Printing - first digit   3 4 5 6 7 8 9 10

Year of Current Printing - first year shown

                2002 2003 2004 2005 2006 2007 2008 2009 2010

Dedicated to my former students

Kerri Baranowski
Laura Butler
Hope Meyers
Lisa O'Quinn
Anne Marie Pepple
Beth Tiefenbrun

Acknowledgments

The readings in this volume are reprinted from the following books by Cardinal Newman.

An Essay on the Development of Christian Doctrine (Garden City: Doubleday, 1960). Used with permission.

Apologia Pro Vita Sua (London, 1924).

Certain Difficulties felt by Anglicans in Catholic Teaching (London, 1885).

Difficulties of Anglicans (London, 1918).

Discourses addressed to Mixed Congregations (New York, 1921).

Discussions and Arguments (London, 1872).

Grammar of Assent (Garden City: Doubleday, 1955). Used with permission.

Historical Sketches (London, 1917).

Lectures on the Doctrine of Justification (London, 1924).

Oxford University Sermons (New York, 1918).

Parochial and Plain Sermons (San Francisco: Ignatius Press, 1987). Used with permission.

Prayers, Verses and Devotions (San Francisco: Ignatius Press, 1989). Used with permission.

Sermons on Subjects of the Day (London, 1902).

Sermons Preached on Various Occasions (London, 1927).

The Arians of the Fourth Century (London, 1888).

The Idea of a University (Garden City: Doubleday, 1959). Used with permission.

COVER PORTRAIT OF CARDINAL NEWMAN BY FRANK SZAZ, KANSAS CITY, MISSOURI. USED WITH PERMISSION.

Contents

I. Knowing God in This Life

II. Evil

III. Self

IV. Liberal Education

V. Death

VI. Heaven

VII. Happiness

VIII. Sin

IX. Grace

X. Faith

XI. God's Love for Us

XII. Our Love for God

XIII. Love of Neighbor

XIV. Use of Creatures

XV. Our Purpose in Life

XVI. Peace

XVII. Prayer

XVIII. Christ

XIX. Church

XX. Mass

XXI. Mary

XXII. Second Coming of Christ

Preface

Of the many avenues — the orator, the writer, the theologian — leading to the treasure house of Newman's profound thoughts, I choose to follow the avenue of image maker. Accordingly, *Newman for Everyone* is a collection of passages in which Newman illustrates his theories by concrete images. I have formulated a question before each selection and arranged the 101 questions according to topics.

This book displays Newman's skill in harmonizing the theoretical with the actual, the abstract with the concrete. It also shows how Newman translates notional assent, the abstract, into real assent, the concrete.

My hope is that readers enjoying *Newman for Everyone* may want to read Newman's complete works: *Apologia Pro Vita Sua*, *The Idea of a University*, *Parochial and Plain Sermons*, etc.

These readings, crafted with such beauty, may suggest either subjects for meditations or themes for homilies.

John Henry Newman (1801-1890) was born in London and studied at Oxford, where he was elected a Fellow of Oriel College. In 1825 he was ordained an Anglican priest. He became a leader of the Oxford Movement, which promoted Catholic tendencies in the Anglican Church. Newman was received into the Roman Catholic Church in 1845, and was ordained a Catholic priest in 1847. In the following year, he founded the first English Oratory in Birmingham. In 1864, in response to a charge of insincerity, Newman wrote his classic account of his spiritual development, the *Apologia Pro Vita Sua*. Pope Leo XIII made him a Cardinal in 1879. Newman was active as a preacher, apologist, theologian, philosopher, historian, poet, novelist, and editor. Besides the *Apologia* and his sermons, his major works include *An Essay on the Development of Christian Doctrine*, *The Idea of a University*, and *The Grammar of Assent*. Newman combined intellectual brilliance with sanctity of life. A movement exists to promote his cause for canonization, and Pope Pius XII once predicted that someday Newman would be declared a Doctor of the Church.

· I ·

Knowing God in This Life

1. Can a child of five or six years old, when reason is at length fully awake, know there is a God?

It is my wish to take an ordinary child, but still one who is safe from influences destructive of his religious instincts. Supposing he has offended his parents, he will all alone and without effort, as if it were the most natural of acts, place himself in the presence of God, and beg of Him to set him right with them. Let us consider how much is contained in this simple act. First, it involves the impression on his mind of an unseen Being with whom he is in immediate relation, and that relation so familiar that he can address Him whenever he himself chooses; next, of One whose goodwill towards him he is assured of, and can take for granted — nay, who loves him better, and is nearer to him, than his parents; further, of One who can hear him, wherever he happens to be, and who can read his thoughts, for his prayer need not be vocal; lastly, of One who can effect a critical change in the state of feeling of others towards him. That is, we shall not be wrong in holding that this child has in his mind the image of an Invisible Being, who exercises a particular providence among us, who is present everywhere, who is heart-reading, heart-changing, ever-accessible, open to impetration. What a strong and intimate vision of God must he have already attained, if, as I have supposed, an ordinary trouble of mind has the spontaneous effect of leading him for consolation and aid to an invisible Personal Power!

Grammar of Assent, pp. 103-104.

2. *Does the voice of conscience echo the Divine Voice?*

Every religious mind, under every dispensation of Providence, will be in the habit of looking out of and beyond self, as regards all matters connected with its highest good. For a man of religious mind is he who attends to the rule of conscience, which is born within him, which he did not make for himself, and to which he feels bound in duty to submit. And conscience immediately directs his thoughts to some Being exterior to himself, who gave it, and who evidently is superior to him; for a law implies a lawgiver, and a command implies a superior. Thus a man is at once thrown out of himself, by the very Voice which speaks within him; and while he rules his heart and conduct by his inward sense of right and wrong, not by the maxims of the external world, still that inward sense does

not allow him to rest in itself, but sends him forth
again from home to seek abroad for Him who
has put His Word in him. He looks forth into
the world to seek Him who is not of the world,
to find behind the shadows and deceits of this
shifting scene of time and sense, Him whose
Word is eternal, and whose Presence is spiritual.

> "Faith without Sight," *Parochial and
> Plain Sermons,* pp. 236-237.

3. *Does created beauty reflect Divine Beauty?*

Leave, then, the prison of your own reasonings,
leave the town, the work of man, the haunt of
sin; go forth, my Brethren, far from the tents of
Cedar and the slime of Babylon: with the patri-
arch go forth to meditate in the field, and from
the splendors of the work imagine the unimag-
inable glory of the Architect. Mount some bold
eminence, and look back, when the sun is high
and full upon the earth, when mountains, cliffs,
and sea rise up before you like a brilliant pageant, with outlines noble and graceful, and tints
and shadows soft, clear, and harmonious, giving depth, and unity to the whole; and then go
through the forest, or fruitful field, or along
meadow and stream, and listen to the distant
country sounds, and drink in the fragrant air
which is poured around you in spring or summer; or go among the gardens, and delight your
senses with the grace and splendor, and the vari-

ous sweetness of the flowers you find there; then think of the almost mysterious influence upon the mind of particular scents, or the emotion which some gentle, peaceful strain excites in us, or how soul and body are rapt and carried away captive by the concord of musical sounds, when the ear is open to their power; and then, when you have ranged through sights, and sounds, and odors, and your heart kindles, and your voice is full of praise and worship, reflect — not that they tell you nothing of their Maker — but that they are the poorest and dimmest glimmerings of His glory, and the very refuse of His exuberant riches, and but the dusky smoke which precedes the flame, compared with Him Who made them. Such is the Creator in His Eternal Uncreated Beauty, that, were it given to us to behold it, we should die of very rapture at the sight.

> "The Mystery of Divine Condescension," *Discourses Addressed to Mixed Congregations*, pp. 296-297.

4. How does the world manifest tokens of God's presence?

How then, it may be asked, can this world have upon it tokens of His presence, or bring us near to Him? Yet certainly so it is, that in spite of the world's evil, after all, He is in it and speaks through it, though not loudly. When He came in the flesh "He was in the world, and the world was made by Him, and the world knew Him not." Nor did He strive nor cry, nor lift up His voice in the streets. So it is now. He is still here; He still whispers to us, He still makes signs to us. But His voice is so low, and the world's din is so loud, and His signs are so covert, and the world is so restless, that it is difficult to determine when He addresses us, and what He says. Religious men cannot but feel, in various ways, that His Providence is guiding them and blessing them personally, on the whole; yet when they attempt to put their finger upon the times and places, the traces of His presence disappear. Who is there, for instance, but has been favoured with answers to prayer, such that, at the time, he has felt he never could again be unbelieving? Who has not had strange coincidences in his course of life which brought before him, in an overpowering way, the hand of God? Who has not had thoughts come upon him with a sort of mysterious force for his warning or his direction? And some persons, perhaps, experience stranger things still. Wonderful providences have before now been brought about by means of dreams; or in other still more unusual ways Almighty God has at times interposed. And then, again, things which come before our eyes, in such wise take the form of types and omens of things moral or future, that the spirit within us cannot but reach forward and presage what it is not told from what it sees. And sometimes these presages are remarkably fulfilled in the event. And then, again, the fortunes of men are so singularly various, as if a law of success and prosperity embraced a certain number, and a contrary law others. All this being so, and the vastness and mystery of the world being borne in upon us, we may well begin to think that there is nothing here below but, for what we know, has a connection with everything else; the most distant events may yet be united, the meanest and the highest may be parts of one; and God may be teaching us and offering us knowledge of His ways, if we will but open our eyes, in all the ordinary matters of the day.

"Waiting for Christ," *Parochial and Plain Sermons*, pp. 1330-1331.

5. *Is the visible world a screen between us and God?*

Oh that there were such an heart in us, to put aside this visible world, to desire to look at it as a mere screen between us and God, and to think of Him who has entered in beyond the veil, and who is watching us, trying us, yes, and bless-ing, and influencing, and encouraging us to-wards good, day by day! Yet, alas, how do we suffer the mere varying circumstances of every day to sway us! How difficult it is to remain firm and in one mind under the seductions or terrors of the world! We feel variously according to the

place, time, and people we are with. We are serious on Sunday, and we sin deliberately on
Monday. We rise in the morning with remorse
at our offenses and resolutions of amendment,
yet before night we have transgressed again. The
mere change of society puts us into a new frame
of mind; nor do we sufficiently understand this
great weakness of ours, or seek for strength
where alone it can be found, in the Unchangeable God. What will be our thoughts in that day,
when at length this outward world drops away
altogether, and we find ourselves where we ever
have been, in His presence, with Christ standing at His right hand!

> "The Immortality of the Soul," *Parochial and
> Plain Sermons*, p. 20.

6. *What does Theology teach us about God?*

I simply mean the science of God, or the truths
we know about God put into system; just as we
have a science of the stars, and call it astronomy,
or of the crust of the earth, and call it geology.

For instance, I mean, for this is the main
point, that, as in the human frame there is a living principle, acting upon it and through it by
means of volition, so, behind the veil of the visible universe, there is an invisible, intelligent
Being, acting on and through it, as and when
He will. Further, I mean that this invisible Agent
is in no sense a soul of the world, after the anal-

ogy of human nature, but, on the contrary, is absolutely distinct from the world, as being its Creator, Upholder, Governor, and Sovereign Lord. Here we are at once brought into the circle of doctrines which the idea of God embodies. I mean then by the Supreme Being one who is simply self-dependent, and the only Being who is such; moreover, that He is without beginning or Eternal, and the only Eternal; that in consequence He has lived a whole eternity by Himself; and hence that He is all-sufficient, sufficient for His own blessedness, and all-blessed, and ever-blessed. Further, I mean a Being, who, having these prerogatives, has the Supreme Good, or rather is the Supreme Good, or has all the attributes of Good in infinite intenseness; all wisdom, all truth, all justice, all love, all holiness, all beautifulness; who is omnipotent, omniscient, omnipresent; ineffably one, absolutely perfect; and such, that what we do not know and cannot even imagine of Him, is far more wonderful than what we do and can. I mean One who is sovereign over His own will and actions, though always according to the eternal Rule of right and wrong, which is Himself. I mean, moreover, that He created all things out of nothing, and preserves them every moment, and could destroy them as easily as He made them; and that, in consequence, He is separated from them by an abyss, and is incommunicable in all His attributes. And further, He has stamped upon all things, in the hour of their creation, their respective natures, and has given them their work and mission and their length of days, greater or less, in their appointed place. I mean, too, that He is ever present with His works, one by one, and confronts everything He has made by His particular and most loving Providence, and manifests Himself to each according to its needs; and has on rational beings imprinted the moral law, and given them power to obey it, imposing on them the duty of worship and service, searching and scanning them through and through with His omniscient eye, and putting before them a present trial and a judgment to come.

The Idea of a University, pp. 96-97.

7. *Might coincidence manifest God's Providence?*

And if a Pope excommunicates a great conqueror; and he, on hearing the threat, says to one of his friends, "Does he think the world has gone back a thousand years? does he suppose the arms will fall from the hands of my soldiers?" and within two years, on retreat over the snows of Russia, as two contemporary historians relate, "famine and cold tore their arms from the grasp of the soldiers," "they fell from the hands of the bravest and most robust," and "destitute of the power of raising them from the ground, the soldiers left them in the snow"; is not this too, though no miracle, a coincidence so special, as rightly to be called a Divine judgment?

Grammar of Assent, p. 332.

8. *What truths are in every religion all over the world?*

We know well enough for practical purposes what is meant by Revealed Religion; viz. that it is the doctrine taught in the Mosaic and Christian dispensations, and contained in the Holy Scriptures, and is from God in a sense in which no other doctrine can be said to be from Him. Yet if we would speak correctly, we must confess, on the authority of the Bible itself, that all knowledge of religion is from Him, and not only that which the Bible has transmitted to us. There never was a time when God had not spoken to man, and told him to a certain extent his duty. His injunctions to Noah, the common father of all mankind, is the first recorded fact of the sacred history after the deluge. Accordingly, we are expressly told in the New Testament, that at no time He left Himself without witness in the world, and that in every nation He accepts those who fear and obey Him. It would seem, then, that there is something true and divinely revealed, in every religion all over the earth, overloaded, as it may be, and at times even stifled by the impieties which the corrupt will and understanding of man have incorporated with it.

Such are the doctrines of the power and presence of an invisible God, of His moral law and governance, of the obligation of duty, and the certainty of a just judgment, and of reward and punishment, as eventually dispensed to individuals; so that Revelation, properly speaking, is an universal, not a local gift; and the distinction between the state of Israelites formerly and Christians now, and that of the heathen, is, not that we can, and they cannot attain to future blessedness, but that the Church of God ever has had, and the rest of mankind never have had, authoritative documents of truth, and appointed channels of communication with Him. The word and the sacraments are the characteristic of the elect people of God; but all men have had more or less the guidance of Tradition, in addition to those internal notions of right and wrong which the Spirit has put into the heart of each individual.

The Arians of the Fourth Century, pp. 79-80.

9. *What earthly elements are shadows of Divine Attributes?*

The attributes of God, though intelligible to us on their surface, for from our own sense of mercy and holiness and patience and consistency, we have general notions of the All-merciful and All-holy and All-patient, and of all that is proper to His Essence, — yet, for the very reason that they

are infinite, transcend our comprehension, when
they are dwelt upon, when they are followed
out, and can only be received by faith. They are
dimly shadowed out, in this very respect, by the
great agents which He has created in the material world. What is so ordinary and familiar to
us as the elements, what so simple and level to
us, as their presence and operation? yet how
their character changes, and how they overmas-
ter us, and triumph over us, when they come
upon us in their fullness! The invisible air, how
gentle is it, and intimately ours! we breathe it
momentarily, nor could we live without it; it fans
our cheek, and flows around us, and we move
through it without effort, while it obediently
recedes at every step we take, and obsequiously
pursues us as we go forward. Yet let it come in
its power, and that same silent fluid, which was
just now the servant of our necessity or caprice,
takes us up on its wings with the invisible power
of an Angel, and carries us forth into the regions
of space, and flings us down headlong upon the
earth. Or go to the spring, and draw thence at
your pleasure, from your cup or your pitcher,
in supply of your wants; you have a ready servant, a domestic ever at hand, in large quantity
or in small, to satisfy your thirst, or to purify
you from the dust and mire of the world. But go
from home, reach the coast; and you will see that
same humble element transformed before your
eyes. You were equal to it in its condescension,

but who shall gaze without astonishment at its vast expanse in the bosom of the ocean? who shall hear without awe the dashing of its mighty billows along the beach? who shall without terror feel it heaving under him, and swelling and mounting up, and yawning wide, till he, its very sport and mockery, is thrown to and fro, hither and thither, at the mere mercy of a power which was just now his companion and almost his slave? Or, again, approach the flame: it warms you, and it enlightens you; yet approach not too near, presume not, or it will change its nature. That very element which is so beautiful to look at, so brilliant in its character, so graceful in its figure, so soft and lambent in its motion, will be found in its essence to be of a keen, resistless nature; it tortures, it consumes, it reduces to ashes that of which it was just before the illumination and the life. So it is with the attributes of God; our knowledge of them serves us for our daily welfare; they give us light and warmth and food and guidance and succor; but go forth with Moses upon the mount and let the Lord pass by, or with Elias stand in the desert amid the wind, the earthquake, and the fire, and all is mystery and darkness; all is but a whirling of the reason, and a dazzling of the imagination, and an overwhelming of the feelings, reminding us that we are but mortal men and He is God, and that the outlines which Nature draws for us are not His perfect image, nor to be pronounced inconsis-

tent with those further lights and depths with
which it is invested by Revelation.

> "The Infinitude of the Divine Attributes,"
> *Discourses Addressed to Mixed Congregations,*
> pp. 318-320.

· II ·
Evil

*10. How did Christian martyrs overcome their
persecutors?*

When the persecution raged in Asia, a vast multitude of Christians presented themselves before
the Proconsul, challenging him to proceed
against them. "Poor wretches!" half in contempt
and half in affright, he answered, "if you must
die, cannot you find ropes or precipices for the
purpose!" At Utica, a hundred and fifty Christians of both sexes and all ages were martyrs in
one company. They are said to have been told
to burn incense to an idol, or they should be
thrown into a pit of burning lime; they without
hesitation leapt into it. In Egypt a hundred and
twenty confessors, after having sustained the
loss of eyes or of feet, endured to linger out their
lives in the mines of Palestine and Cilicia. In the
last persecution, according to the testimony of
the grave Eusebius, a contemporary, the slaugh-
ter of men, women, and children, went on by
twenties, sixties, hundreds, till the instruments
of execution were worn out, and the execution-
ers could kill no more. Yet he tells us, as an eye-

witness, that, as soon as any Christians were condemned, others ran from all parts, and surrounded the tribunals, confessing the faith, and joyfully receiving their condemnation, and singing songs of thanksgiving and triumph to the last. Thus was the Roman power overcome.

Grammar of Assent, pp. 373-374.

11. *How did the Benedictine monks conquer the barbarian invaders?*

And then, when they had in the course of many years gained their peaceful victories, perhaps some new invader came, and with fire and sword undid their slow and persevering toil in an hour. The Hun succeeded to the Goth, the Lombard to the Hun, the Tartar to the Lombard; the Saxon was reclaimed only that the Dane might take his place. Down in the dust lay the labor and civilization of centuries — Churches, Colleges, Cloisters, Libraries — and nothing was left to them but to begin all over again; but this they did without grudging, so promptly, cheerfully, and tranquilly, as if it were by some law of nature that the restoration came, and they were like the flowers and shrubs and fruit trees which they reared, and which, when ill-treated, do not take vengeance, or remember evil, but give forth fresh branches, leaves, or blossoms, perhaps in greater profusion, and with richer quality, for the very reason that the old were

rudely broken off. If one holy place was des-
ecrated, the monks pitched upon another, and
by this time there were rich or powerful men
who remembered and loved the past enough to
wish to have it restored in the future. Thus was
it in the case of the monastery of Ramsey after
the ravages of the Danes.

Historical Sketches, Vol. II, pp. 410-411.

12. *How does the devil use the Church to tempt the*
    faithful?

Was it promised to the sons of the Church to do
miracles? Antichrist is to do "lying wonders."
Do they exhibit a meekness and a firmness most
admirable, a marvelous self-denial, a fervency
in prayer, and a charity? It is answered: "This
only makes them more dangerous. Do you not
know that Satan can transform himself into an
angel of light?" Are they, according to our Lord's
bidding, like sheep, defenseless and patient?
This does but fulfill a remarkable prophecy, it is
retorted; for the second beast, which came up
out of the earth, "had two horns like a lamb's,
while it spoke like a dragon." Does the Church
fulfill the Scripture description of being weak
and yet strong, of conquering by yielding, of
having nothing yet gaining all things, and of exercising power without wealth or station? This
wonderful fact, which ought surely to startle the
most obstinate, is assigned, not to the power of

God, but to some political art or conspiracy. Angels walk the earth in vain; to the gross prejudice of the multitude their coming and going is the secret plotting, as they call it, of "monks and Jesuits." Good forsooth it cannot, shall not be; rather believe anything than that it comes from God; believe in a host of invisible traitors prowling about and disseminating doctrine adverse to your own, believe us to be liars and deceivers, men of blood, ministers of hell, rather than turn your minds, by way of solving the problem, to the possibility of our being what we say we are, the children and servants of the true Church. There never was a more successful artifice than this, which the author of evil has devised against his Maker, that God's work is not God's but his own. He has spread this abroad in the world, as thieves in a crowd escape by giving the alarm; and men, in their simplicity, run away from Christ as if Christ were he, and run into his arms as if he were Christ.

"Christ upon the Waters," *Sermons Preached on Various Occasions*, pp. 143-144.

13. How may the disappointments of life prompt us to rejoice?

Such being the unprofitableness of this life, viewed in itself, it is plain how we should regard it while we go through it. We should remember that it is scarcely more than an accident of our being — that it is no part of ourselves, who are immortal; that we are immortal spirits, independent of time and space, and that this life is but a sort of outward stage, on which we act for a time, and which is only sufficient and only intended to answer the purpose of trying whether we will serve God or no. We should consider ourselves to be in this world in no fuller sense than players in any game are in the game; and life to be a sort of dream, as detached and as different from our real eternal existence, as a dream differs from waking; a serious dream, indeed, as affording a means of judging us, yet in itself a kind of shadow without substance, a scene set before us, in which we seem to be, and in which it is our duty to act just as if all we saw had a truth and reality, because all that meets us influences us and our destiny. The regenerate soul is taken into communion with Saints and Angels, and its "life is hid with Christ in God" *Col.* iii. 3; it has a place in God's court, and is not of this world — looking into this world as a spectator might look at some show or pageant, except when called from time to time to take a part. And while it obeys the instinct of the senses, it does so for God's sake, and it submits itself to things of time so far as to be brought to perfection by them, that, when the veil is withdrawn and it sees itself to be, where it ever has been, in God's kingdom, it may be found worthy to enjoy it. It is this view of life, which removes from us all surprise and disappointment that it is so incomplete: as well might we expect any chance event which happens in the course of it to be complete, any casual conversation with a stranger, or the toil or amusement of an hour.

Let us then thus account of our present state: it is precious in revealing to us, amid shadows and figures, the existence and attributes of Almighty God and His elect people: it is precious, because it enables us to hold intercourse with immortal souls who are on their trial as we are. It is momentous, as being the scene and means of our trial; but beyond this it has no claims upon us. "Vanity of vanities, says the Preacher, all is vanity." We may be poor or rich, young or old, honored or slighted, and it ought to affect us no more, neither to elate us nor depress us, than if we were actors in a play, who know that the characters they represent are not their own, and that though they may appear to be superior one to another, to be kings or to be peasants, they are in reality all on a level. The one desire which should move us should be, first of all, that of seeing Him face to face, who is now hid from us; and next of enjoying eternal and direct communion, in and through Him, with our friends around us, whom at present we know only through the medium of sense, by precarious and partial channels, which give us little insight into their hearts.

"The Greatness and Littleness of Human Life,"
Parochial and Plain Sermons, pp. 865-866.

14. *Why does God send us afflictions?*

Without denying, then, to these persons the
praise of many religious habits and practices, I
would say that they want the tender and sensitive heart which hangs on the thought of Christ,
and lives in His love. The breath of the world
has a peculiar power in what may be called rust-
ing the soul. The mirror within them, instead of
reflecting back the Son of God their Saviour, has
become dim and discolored; and hence, though
(to use a common expression) they have a good
deal of good *in* them, it is only *in* them, it is not
through them, around them, and upon them. An
evil crust is *on* them: they think with the world;
they are full of the world's notions and modes
of speaking; they appeal to the world, and have
a sort of reverence for what the world will say.
There is a want of naturalness, simplicity, and
childlike teachableness in them. It is difficult to
touch them, or (what may be called) get at them,
and to persuade them to a straightforward
course in religion. They start off when you least
expect it: they have reservations, make distinc-
tions, take exceptions, indulge in refinements,
in questions where there are really but two sides,
a right and a wrong. Their religious feelings do
not flow forth easily, at times when they ought
to flow; either they are diffident, and can say
nothing, or else they are affected and strained
in their mode of conversing! And as a rust preys
upon metal and eats into it, so does this worldly

spirit penetrate more and more deeply into the
soul which once admits it. And this is one great
end, as it would appear, of afflictions, viz. to rub
away and clear off these outward defilements,
and to keep the soul in a measure of its baptis-
mal purity and brightness.

"Watching," *Parochial and Plain Sermons*, pp. 935-936.

15. *How may God call us to lead a better life?*

Perhaps it may be the loss of some dear friend
or relative through which the call comes to us;
which shows us the vanity of things below, and
prompts us to make God our sole stay. We
through grace do so in a way we never did before; and in the course of years, when we look
back on our life, we find that that sad event has
brought us into a new state of faith and judgment, and that we are as though other men from
which we were. We thought, before it took place,
that we were serving God, and so we were in a
measure; but we find that, whatever our present
infirmities may be, and however far we be still
from the highest state of illumination, then at
least we were serving the world under the show
and the belief of serving God.

"Divine Calls," *Parochial and Plain Sermons*, p. 1572.

16. *Are those who uphold Divine Truth exposed to the charge of singularity?*

No; there are numberless clouds which flit over

the sky, there are numberless gusts which agitate the air to and fro: as many, as violent, as far-spreading, as fleeting, as uncertain, as changing, are the clouds and the gales of human opinion; as suddenly, as impetuously, as fruitlessly, do they assail those whose mind is stayed on God. They come and they go; they have no life in them, or abidance. They agree together in nothing but in this, in threatening like clouds, and sweeping like gusts of wind. They are the voice of the many; they have the strength of the world, and they are directed against the few. Their argument, the sole argument in their behalf, is their prevalence at the moment; not that they existed yesterday, not that they will exist tomorrow; not that they base themselves on reason, or ancient belief, but that they are merely what every one now takes for granted, or, perhaps, supposes to be in Scripture, and therefore not to be disputed: — not that they have most voices through long periods, but that they happen to be most numerously professed in the passing hour. On the other hand, Divine Truth is ever one and the same; it changes not, any more than its Author: it stands to reason, then, that those who uphold it must ever be exposed to the charge of singularity, either for this or for that portion of it, in a world which is ever varying.

"Many called, Few chosen," *Parochial and Plain Sermons*, p. 1117.

· III ·

Self

17. *What is an argument for the immortality of the soul?*

"I think," says the poor dying factory girl in the tale ('North and South'), "if this should be the end of all, and if all I have been born for is just to work my heart and life away, and to sicken in this dree place, with those millstones in my ears for ever, until I could scream out for them to stop and let me have a little piece of quiet, and with the fluff filling my lungs, until I thirst to death for one long deep breath of the clear air, and my mother gone, and I never able to tell her again how I loved her, and of all my troubles — I think, if this life is the end, and that there is no God to wipe away all tears from all eyes, I could go mad!"

Grammar of Assent, p. 247.

18. *How does the feebleness of created things help us come to have a glimpse of the meaning of our immortality?*

We look off from self to the things around us, and forget ourselves in them. Such is our state

— a depending for support on the reeds which
are no stay, and overlooking our real strength
— at the time when God begins His process of
reclaiming us to a truer view of our place in His
great system of providence. And when He vis-
its us, then in a little while there is a stirring
within us. The unprofitableness and feebleness
of the things of this world are forced upon our
minds; they promise but cannot perform, they
disappoint us. Or, if they do perform what they
promise, still (so it is) they do not satisfy us. We
still crave for something, we do not well know
what; but we are sure it is something which the
world has not given us. And then its changes
are so many, so sudden, so silent, so continual.
It never leaves changing; it goes on to change,
till we are quite sick at heart: — then it is that
our reliance on it is broken. It is plain we cannot
continue to depend upon it unless we keep pace
with it and go on changing too; but this we cannot do. We feel that, while it changes, we are
one and the same; and thus, under God's blessing, we come to have some glimpse of the meaning of our independence of things temporal, and
our immortality. And should it so happen that
misfortunes come upon us (as they often do),
then still more are we led to understand the noth-
ingness of this world; then still more are we led
to distrust it, and are weaned from the love of it,
till at length it floats before our eyes merely as
some idle veil of what is beyond it; — and we

begin, by degrees, to perceive that there are but two beings in the whole universe, our own soul and the God who made it.

"The Immortality of the Soul," *Parochial and Plain Sermons*, pp. 16-17.

19. Why is it dangerous to separate feeling and acting?

God has made us feel in order that we may *go on to act* in consequence of feeling; if then we allow our feelings to be excited without acting upon them, we do mischief to the moral system within us, just as we might spoil a watch, or other piece of mechanism, by playing with the wheels of it. We weaken its springs, and they cease to act truly.

"The Danger of Accomplishments," *Parochial and Plain Sermons*, p. 459.

20. What is a method of calming an agitated mind?

It has sometimes been well suggested, as a mode of calming the mind when set upon an object, or much vexed or angered at some occurrence, what will you feel about all this a year hence? It is very plain that matters which agitate us most extremely now, will then interest us not at all; that objects about which we have intense hope and fear now, will then be to us nothing more than things which happen at the other end of the earth. So will it be with all human hopes, fears, pleasures, pains, jealousies, disappointments, successes, when the last day is come. They will have no life in them; they will be as the faded flowers of a banquet, which do but mock us. Or when we lie on the bed of death, what will it avail us to have been rich, or great, or fortunate, or honoured, or influential? All things will then be vanity. Well, what this world will be understood by all to be then, such is it felt to be by the Christian now. He looks at things as he then will look at them, with an uninterested and dispassionate eye, and is neither pained much nor pleased much at the accidents of life, because they are accidents.

> "Equanimity," *Parochial and Plain Sermons*,
> p. 991.

· IV ·

Liberal Education

21. Why do university students need teachers?

The general principles of any study you may learn by books at home; but the detail, the colour, the tone, the air, the life which makes it live in us, you must catch all these from those in whom it lives already. You must imitate the student in French or German, who is not content with his grammar, but goes to Paris or Dresden: you must take example from the young artist, who aspires to visit the great Masters in Florence and in Rome. Till we have discovered some intellectual daguerreotype, which takes off the course of thought, and the form, lineaments, and features of truth, as completely, and minutely, as the optical instrument produces the sensible object, we must come to the teachers of wisdom to learn wisdom; we must repair to the fountain, and drink there. Portions may go from thence to the ends of the earth by means of books; but the fullness is in one place alone. It is in such assemblages and congregations of intellect that books

themselves, the masterpieces of human genius,
are written, or at least originated.

Historical Sketches, Vol. III, p. 9.

22. *Should teachers have a personal influence on
their students?*

An academical system without the personal influence of teachers upon pupils, is an arctic winter; it will create an ice-bound, petrified, cast-
iron university, and nothing else. You will not
call this any new notion of mine; and you will
not suspect, after what happened to me a long
twenty-five years ago, that I can never be in-
duced to think otherwise. No! I have known a
time in a great School of Letters, when things
went on for the most part by mere routine, and
form took the place of earnestness. I have expe-
rienced a state of things, in which teachers were
cut off from the taught as by an insurmountable
barrier; when neither party entered into the
thoughts of the other; when each lived by and
in itself; when the tutor was supposed to fulfil
his duty, if he trotted on like a squirrel in his
cage, if at a certain hour he was in a certain room,
or in hall, or in chapel, as it might be; and the
pupil did his duty too, if he was careful to meet
his tutor in that same room, or hall, or chapel, at
the same certain hour; and when neither the one
nor the other dreamed of seeing each other out
of lecture, out of chapel, out of academical gown.

I have known places where a still manner, a
pompous voice, coldness and condescension,
were the teacher's attributes, and where he neither knew, nor wished to know, and avowed he
did not wish to know, the private irregularities
of the youths committed to his charge.

Historical Sketches, Vol. III, pp. 74-75.

23. *What should be the integrating principle of a Catholic university?*

All we see, hear, and touch, the remote sidereal
firmament, as well as our own sea and land, and
the elements which compose them, and the ordinances they obey, are His. The primary atoms
of matter, their properties, their mutual action,
their disposition and collocation, electricity,
magnetism, gravitation, light, and whatever
other subtle principles or operations the wit of
man is detecting or shall detect, are the work of
His hands. From Him has been every movement
which has convulsed and refashioned the surface of the earth. The most insignificant or un-
sightly insect is from Him, and good in its kind;
the ever-teeming, inexhaustible swarms of
animalculae, the myriads of living motes invisible to the naked eye, the restless, ever-spread-
ing vegetation which creeps like a garment over
the whole earth, the lofty cedar, the umbrageous
banana, are His. His are the tribes and families

of birds and beasts, their graceful forms, their wild gestures, and their passionate cries.

And so in the intellectual, moral, social, and political world. Man, with his motives and works, his languages, his propagation, his diffusion is from Him. Agriculture, medicine, and the arts of life are His gifts. Society, laws, government, He is their sanction.

The Idea of a University, p. 98.

24. *What is the elementary idea of science and philosophy?*

One of the first acts of the human mind is to take hold of and appropriate what meets the senses, and herein lies a chief distinction between man's and brute's use of them. Brutes gaze on sights, they are arrested by sounds; and what they see and what they hear are mainly sights and sounds only. The intellect of man, on the contrary, energizes as well as his eye or ear, and perceives in sights and sounds something beyond them. It seizes and unites what the senses present to it; it grasps and forms what need not have been seen or heard except in its constituent parts. It discerns in lines and colours, or in tones, what is beautiful and what is not. It gives them a meaning, and invests them with an idea. It gathers up a succession of notes into the expression of a whole and calls it a melody; it has a keen

sensibility towards angles and curves, lights and
shadows, tints and contours. It distinguishes
between rule and exception, between accident
and design. It assigns phenomena to a general
law, qualities to a subject, acts to a principle, and
effects to a cause. In a word, it philosophizes;
for I suppose science and philosophy, in their
elementary idea, are nothing else but this habit
of *viewing*, as it may be called, the objects which
sense conveys to the mind, of throwing them into
a system, and uniting and stamping them with
one form.

The Idea of a University, pp. 106-107.

25. Are all branches of knowledge interconnected?

I have said that all branches of knowledge are
connected together, because the subject matter
of knowledge is intimately united in itself, as
being the acts and work of the Creator. Hence it
is that the sciences, into which our knowledge
may be said to be cast, have multiplied bearings
one on another, and an internal sympathy, and
admit, or rather demand, comparison and ad-
justment. They complete, correct, balance each
other. This consideration, if well founded, must
be taken into account, not only as regards the
attainment of truth, which is their common end,
but as regards the influence which they exercise
upon those whose education consists in the

study of them. I have said already that to give undue prominence to one is to be unjust to another; to neglect or supersede these is to divert those from their proper object. It is to unsettle the boundary lines between science and science, to disturb their action, to destroy the harmony which binds them together. Such a proceeding will have a corresponding effect when introduced into a place of education. There is no science but tells a different tale, when viewed as a portion of a whole, from what it is likely to suggest when taken by itself, without the safeguard, as I may call it, of others.

Let me make use of an illustration. In the combination of colours, very different effects are produced by a difference in their selection and juxtaposition; red, green, and white change their shades, according to the contrast to which they are submitted. And, in like manner, the drift and meaning of a branch of knowledge varies with the company in which it is introduced to the student. If his reading is confined simply to one subject, however such division of labour may favour the advancement of a particular pursuit, a point into which I do not here enter, certainly it has a tendency to contract his mind. If it is incorporated with others, it depends on those others as to the kind of influence which it exerts upon him.

The Idea of a University, pp. 127-128.

26. *Does philosophy harness the passions and the pride of human beings?*

Knowledge is one thing, virtue is another; good sense is not conscience, refinement is not humility, nor is largeness and justness of view faith. Philosophy, however enlightened, however profound, gives no command over the passions, no influential motives, no vivifying principles. Liberal education makes not the Christian, not the Catholic, but the gentleman. It is well to be a gentleman, it is well to have a cultivated intellect, a delicate taste, a candid, equitable, dispassionate mind, a noble and courteous bearing in the conduct of life; these are the connatural qualities of a large knowledge; they are the objects of a university; I am advocating, I shall illustrate and insist upon them; but still, I repeat, they are no guarantee for sanctity or even for conscientiousness; they may attach to the man of the world, to the profligate, to the heartless — pleasant, alas, and attractive as he shows when decked out in them. Taken by themselves, they do but seem to be what they are not; they look like virtue at a distance, but they are detected by close observers, and on the long run; and hence it is that they are popularly accused of pretence and hypocrisy, not, I repeat, from their own fault, but because their professors and their admirers persist in taking them for what they are not, and are officious in arrogating for them a praise to which they have no claim. Quarry the granite rock with razors, or moor the vessel with a thread of silk; then may you hope with such keen and delicate instruments as human knowledge and human reason to contend against those giants, the passion and the pride of man.

The Idea of a University, pp. 144-145.

27. *What is a liberal education in itself?*

Surely it is very intelligible to say, and that is what I say here, that liberal education, viewed in itself, is simply the cultivation of the intellect, as such, and its object is nothing more or less than intellectual excellence. Everything has its own perfection, be it higher or lower in the scale of things; and the perfection of one is not the perfection of another. Things animate, inanimate, visible, invisible, all are good in their kind, and have a *best* of themselves, which is an object of pursuit. Why do you take such pains with your garden or your park? You see to your walks and turf and shrubberies; to your trees and drives; not as if you meant to make an orchard of the one, or corn or pastureland of the other, but because there is a special beauty in all that is goodly in wood, water, plain, and slope, brought all together by art into one shape, and grouped into one whole. Your cities are beautiful, your palaces, your public buildings, your territorial mansions, your churches; and their beauty leads to nothing beyond itself. There is a physical beauty and a moral: there is a beauty of person, there is a beauty of our moral being, which is natural virtue; and in like manner there is a beauty, there is a perfection, of the intellect. There is an ideal perfection in these various subject matters, towards which individual instances are seen to rise, and which are the standards for all instances whatever. The Greek divinities and demigods, as the statuary has moulded them, with their symmetry of figure, and their high forehead and their regular features, are the perfection of physical beauty. The heroes, of whom history tells, Alexander, or Caesar, or Scipio, or Saladin, are the representatives of that magnanimity or self-mastery which is the greatness of human nature. Christianity too has its heroes, and in the supernatural order, and we call them saints. The artist puts before him beauty of feature and form; the poet, the beauty of mind; the preacher, the beauty of grace: then intellect too, I repeat, has its beauty, and it has those who aim at it. To open the mind, to correct it, to refine it, to enable it to know, and to digest, master, rule, and use its knowledge, to give it power over its own faculties, application, flexibility, method, critical exactness, sagacity, resource, address, eloquent expression, is an object as intelligible (for here we are inquiring, not what the object of a liberal education is worth, nor what use the Church makes of it, but what it is in itself), I say,

an object as intelligible as the cultivation of virtue, while, at the same time, it is absolutely distinct from it.

The Idea of a University, pp. 145-146.

28. *What is the bare idea of a university?*

In default of a recognized term, I have called the
perfection or virtue of the intellect by the name
of philosophy, philosophical knowledge, en-
largement of mind, or illumination, terms which
are not uncommonly given to it by writers of
this day: but whatever name we bestow on it, it
is, I believe, as a matter of history, the business
of a university to make this intellectual culture
its direct scope, or to employ itself in the education of the intellect — just as the work of a hos-
pital lies in healing the sick or wounded, of a
riding or fencing school, or of a gymnasium, in
exercising the limbs, of an almshouse, in aiding
and solacing the old, of an orphanage, in pro-
tecting innocence, of a penitentiary, in restoring
the guilty. I say, a university, taken in its bare
idea, and before we view it as an instrument of
the Church, has this object and this mission; it
contemplates neither moral impression nor me-
chanical production; it professes to exercise the
mind neither in art nor in duty; its function is
intellectual culture; here it may leave its schol-
ars, and it has done its work when it has done
as much as this. It educates the intellect to rea-

son well in all matters, to reach out towards
truth, and to grasp it.

The Idea of a University, p. 149.

29. Does the mere acquisition of facts and theories constitute a liberal education, a philosophy?

In like manner, we sometimes fall in with persons who have seen much of the world, and of
the men who, in their day, have played a con-
spicuous part in it, but who generalize nothing,
and have no observation, in the true sense of the
word. They abound in information in detail,
curious and entertaining, about men and things;
having lived under the influence of no very clear
or settled principles, religious or political, they
speak of every one and every thing, only as so
many phenomena, which are complete in themselves, and lead to nothing, not discussing them,
or teaching any truth, or instructing the hearer,
but simply talking. No one would say that these
persons, well informed as they are, had attained
to any great culture of intellect or to philosophy.

The case is the same still more strikingly
where the persons in question are beyond dis-
pute men of inferior powers and deficient education. Perhaps they have been much in foreign
countries, and they receive, in a passive, otiose,
unfruitful way, the various facts which are
forced upon them there. Seafaring men, for example, range from one end of the earth to the

other; but the multiplicity of external objects which they have encountered forms no symmetrical and consistent picture upon their imagination; they see the tapestry of human life, as it were on the wrong side, and it tells no story. They sleep, and they rise up, and they find themselves, now in Europe, now in Asia; they see visions of great cities and wild regions; they are in the marts of commerce, or amid the islands of the South; they gaze on Pompey's Pillar, or on the Andes; and nothing which meets them carries them forward or backward to any idea beyond itself. Nothing has a drift or relation; nothing has a history or a promise. Everything stands by itself, and comes and goes in its turn, like the shifting scenes of a show, which leave the spectator where he was. Perhaps you are near such a man on a particular occasion, and expect him to be shocked or perplexed at something which occurs; but one thing is much the same to him as another, or, if he is perplexed, it is as not knowing what to say, whether it is right to admire, or to ridicule, or to disapprove, while conscious that some expression of opinion is expected from him; for in fact he has no standard of judgment at all, and no landmarks to guide him to a conclusion. Such is mere acquisition, and, I repeat, no one would dream of calling it philosophy.

The Idea of a University, pp. 157-158.

*30. Does thought exercised upon knowledge
    seeking a comprehensive view of reality
    constitute a liberal education, a philosophy?*

That perfection of the intellect, which is the result of education, and its *beau ideal*, is the clear,
accurate vision and comprehension of all things,
as far as the finite mind can embrace them, each
in its place, and with its own characteristics upon
it. It is almost prophetic from its knowledge of
history; it has almost supernatural charity from
its freedom from littleness and prejudice; it has
almost the repose of faith, because nothing can
startle it; it has almost the beauty and harmony
of heavenly contemplation, so intimate is it with
the eternal order of things and the music of the
spheres.

And now, if I may take for granted that the
true and adequate end of intellectual training
and of a university is not learning or acquire-
ment, but rather is thought or reason exercised
upon knowledge, or what may be called philosophy, I shall be in a position to explain the various mistakes which at the present day beset the
subject of university education.

I say then, if we would improve the intellect, first of all we must ascend; we cannot gain
real knowledge on a level; we must generalize,
we must reduce to method, we must have a
grasp of principles, and group and shape our
acquisitions by means of them. It matters not
whether our field of operation be wide or lim-

ited; in every case, to command it, is to mount above it. Who has not felt the irritation of mind and impatience created by a deep, rich country, visited for the first time, with winding lanes, and high hedges, and green steeps, and tangled woods, and everything smiling indeed, but in a maze? The same feeling comes upon us in a strange city, when we have no map of its streets. Hence you hear of practised travellers, when they first come into a place, mounting some high hill or church tower, by way of reconnoitering its neighborhood. In like manner, you must be above your knowledge, not under it, or it will oppress you; and the more you have of it, the greater will be the load. The learning of a Salmasius or a Burman, unless you are its master, will be your tyrant. "He commands or he obeys"; if you can wield it with a strong arm, it is a great weapon; otherwise,

> Destitute of the force of advice
> He falls by his own weight.

You will be overwhelmed, like Tarpeia, by the heavy wealth which you have exacted from tributary generations.

The Idea of a University, pp. 160-161.

31. *What is the business of a university?*

The bodily eye, the organ for apprehending material objects, is provided by nature; the eye of the mind, of which the object is truth, is the work of discipline.

This process of training, by which the intellect, instead of being formed or sacrificed to some particular or accidental purpose, some specific trade or profession, or study or science, is disciplined for its own sake, for the perception of its own proper object, and for its own highest culture, is called liberal education; and though there is no one in whom it is carried as far as is conceivable, or whose intellect would be a pattern of what intellects should be made, yet there is scarcely anyone but may gain an idea of what real training is, and at least look towards it, and make its true scope and result, not something else, his standard of excellence; and numbers there are who may submit themselves to it, and secure it to themselves in good measure. And to set forth the right standard, and to train according to it, and to help forward all students towards it according to their various capacities, this I conceive to be the business of a university.

The Idea of a University, p. 171.

32. *What is the definition of a gentleman?*

Hence it is that it is almost a definition of a gentleman to say he is one who never inflicts pain. This description is both refined and, as far as it goes, accurate. He is mainly occupied in merely removing the obstacles which hinder the

free and unembarrassed action of those about
him; and he concurs with their movements
rather than takes the initiative himself. His benefits may be considered as parallel to what are
called comforts or conveniences in arrangements
of a personal nature: like an easy chair or a good
fire, which do their part in dispelling cold and
fatigue, though nature provides both means of
rest and animal heat without them. The true
gentleman in like manner carefully avoids whatever may cause a jar or a jolt in the minds of
those with whom he is cast — all clashing of
opinion, or collision of feeling, all restraint, or
suspicion, or gloom, or resentment; his great
concern being to make every one at their ease
and at home. He has his eyes on all his company; he is tender towards the bashful, gentle
towards the distant, and merciful towards the
absurd; he can recollect to whom he is speaking; he guards against unseasonable allusions,
or topics which may irritate; he is seldom promi-
nent in conversation, and never wearisome; he
makes light of favours while he does them, and
seems to be receiving when he is conferring. He
never speaks of himself except when compelled,
never defends himself by a mere retort, he has
no ears for slander or gossip, is scrupulous in
imputing motives to those who interfere with
him, and interprets everything for the best. He
is never mean or little in his disputes, never takes
unfair advantage, never mistakes personalities

or sharp sayings for arguments, or insinuates evil which he dare not say out. From a long-sighted prudence, he observes the maxim of the ancient sage that we should ever conduct ourselves towards our enemy as if he were one day to be our friend.

The Idea of a University, pp. 217-218.

33. How did certain authors assist in the formation of the English language?

Certain masters of composition, as Shakespeare, Milton, and Pope, the writers of the Protestant Bible and Prayer Book, Hooker and Addison, Swift, Hume, and Goldsmith, have been the making of the English language; and as that language is a fact, so is the literature a fact, by which it is formed, and in which it lives. Men of great ability have taken it in hand, each in his own day, and have done for it what the master of a gymnasium does for the bodily frame. They have formed its limbs, and developed its strength; they have endowed it with vigour, exercised it in suppleness and dexterity, and taught it grace. They have made it rich, harmonious, various and precise. They have furnished it with a variety of styles, which from their individuality may almost be called dialects, and are monuments both of the powers of the language and the genius of its cultivation.

The Idea of a University, p. 297.

34. *Is the purpose of university education discipline in accuracy of mind?*

The little babe stretches out his arms and fingers, as if to grasp or to fathom the many-coloured vision; and thus he gradually learns the connection of part with part, separates what moves from what is stationary, watches the coming and going of figures, masters the idea of shape and of perspective, calls in the information conveyed through the other senses to assist him in his mental process, and thus gradually converts a kaleidoscope into a picture. The first view was the more splendid, the second the more real; the former more poetical, the latter more philosophical. Alas! what are we doing all through life, both as a necessity and as a duty, but unlearning the world's poetry, and attaining to its prose! This is our education, as boys and as men, in the action of life, and in the closet or library; in our affections, in our aims, in our hopes, and in our memories. And in like manner it is the education of our intellect; I say, that one main portion of intellectual education, of the labours of both school and university, is to remove the original dimness of the mind's eye; to strengthen and perfect its vision; to enable it to look out into the world right forward, steadily and truly; to give the mind clearness, accuracy, precision; to enable it to use words aright, to understand what it says, to conceive justly what it thinks about, to abstract, compare, analyze, divide, define, and reason, correctly. There is a particular science which takes these matters in hand, and it is called logic; but it is not by logic, certainly not by logic alone, that the faculty I speak of is acquired. The infant does not learn to spell and read the hues upon his retinae by any scientific rule; nor does the student learn accuracy of thought by any manual or treatise. The instruction given him, of whatever kind, if it be really instruction, is mainly, or at least preeminently, this — a discipline in accuracy of mind.

The Idea of a University, pp. 312-313.

35. *How does love of reading differ from real study?*

Nothing is more common in an age like this, when books abound, than to fancy that the gratification of a love of reading is real study. Of course there are youths who shrink even from story books, and cannot be coaxed into getting through a tale of romance. Such Mr. Brown was not; but there are others, and I suppose he was in their number, who certainly have a taste for reading but in whom it is little more than the result of mental restlessness and curiosity. Such minds cannot fix their gaze on one object for two seconds together; the very impulse which leads them to read at all, leads them to read on, and never to stay or hang over any one idea. The pleasurable excitement of reading what is new

is their motive principle; and the imagination
that they are doing something, and the boyish
vanity which accompanies it, are their reward.
Such youths often profess to like poetry, or to
like history or biography; they are fond of lectures on certain of the physical sciences; or they
may possibly have a real and true taste for natural history or other cognate subjects — and so
far they may be regarded with satisfaction; but
on the other hand they profess that they do not
like logic, they do not like algebra, they have no
taste for mathematics; which only means that
they do not like application, they do not like attention, they shrink from the effort and labour
of thinking, and the process of true intellectual
gymnastics. The consequence will be that, when
they grow up, they may, if it so happen, be agree-
able in conversation, they may be well informed
in this or that department of knowledge, they
may be what is called literary; but they will have
no consistency, steadiness, or perseverance; they
will not be able make a telling speech, or write a
good letter, or to fling in debate a smart antago-
nist, unless so far as, now and then, mother wit
supplies a sudden capacity, which cannot be
ordinarily counted on. They cannot state an argument or a question, or take a clear survey of a
whole transaction, or give sensible and appropriate advice under difficulties, or do any of
those things which inspire confidence and gain

influence, which raise a man in life, and make
him useful to his religion or his country.

The Idea of a University, pp. 320-321.

36. *How do physics and theology differ?*

Such is physical science, and theology, as is obvious, is just what such science is not. Theology
begins, as its name denotes, not with any sensible facts, phenomena, or results, not with nature at all, but with the Author of nature — with
the one invisible, unapproachable Cause and
Source of all things. It begins at the other end of
knowledge, and is occupied, not with the finite,
but the Infinite. It unfolds and systematizes what
He Himself has told us of Himself; of His nature, His attributes, His will, and His acts. As
far as it approaches towards Physics, it takes just
the counterpart of the questions which occupy
the physical philosopher. He contemplates facts
before him; the theologian gives the reasons of
those facts. The physicist treats of efficient
causes; the theologian of final. The physicist tells
us of laws; the theologian of the Author,
Maintainer, and Controller of them; of their
scope, of their suspension, if so be; of their beginning and their end. This is how the two
schools stand related to each other, at that point
where they approach the nearest; but for the
most part they are absolutely divergent. What
physical science is engaged in I have already

said; as to theology, it contemplates the world, not of matter, but of mind; the Supreme Intelligence; souls and their destiny; conscience and duty; the past, present, and future dealings of the Creator with the creature.

So far, then, as these remarks have gone, theology and physics cannot touch each other, have no intercommunion, have no ground of difference or agreement, of jealousy or of sympathy. As well may musical truths be said to interfere with the doctrines of architectural science; as well may there be a collision between the mechanist and the geologist, the engineer and the grammarian; as well might the British Parliament or the French nation be jealous of some possible belligerent power upon the surface of the moon, as physics pick a quarrel with theology.

The Idea of a University, p. 395.

37. *Are the moral law and the truths of faith as evident to us as the truths of physical science?*

The reflection of sky and mountains in the lake is a proof that sky and mountains are around it, but the twilight, or the mist, or the sudden storm hurries away the beautiful image, which leaves behind it no memorial of what it was. Something like this are the moral law and the informations of faith, as they present themselves to individual minds. Who can deny the existence of conscience? who does not feel the force of its injunctions? but how dim is the illumination in which it is invested, and how feeble its influence, compared with the evidence of sight and touch which is the foundation of physical science! How easily can we be talked out of our clearest views of duty! how does this or that moral precept crumble into nothing when we rudely handle it! how does the fear of sin pass off from us, as quickly as the glow of modesty dies away from the countenance! and then we say, "It is all superstition." However, after a time we look round, and then to our surprise we see, as before, the same law of duty, the same moral precepts, the same protests against sin, appearing over against us, in their old places, as if they never had been brushed away, like the divine handwriting upon the wall at the banquet. Then perhaps we approach them rudely, and inspect them irreverently, and accost them skeptically, and away they go again, like so many specters — shining in their cold beauty, but not presenting themselves bodily to us, for our inspection, so to say, of their hands and their feet. And thus these awful, supernatural, bright, majestic, delicate apparitions, much as we may in our hearts acknowledge their sovereignty, are no match as a foundation of science for the hard, palpable, material facts which make up the province of physics.

The Idea of a University , pp. 460-461.

· V ·

Death

38. How may Christ's conduct at the time of Lazarus' death assist us at the time of our own death?

Let us take to ourselves these comfortable thoughts, both in the contemplation of our own death, or upon the death of our friends. Wherever faith in Christ is, there is Christ Himself. He said to Martha, "Believest thou this?" Wherever there is a heart to answer, "Lord, I believe," there Christ is present. There our Lord vouchsafes to stand, though unseen — whether over the bed of death or over the grave; whether we ourselves are sinking or those who are dear to us. Blessed be His name! nothing can rob us of this consolation: we will be as certain, through His grace, that He is standing over us in love, as though we saw Him. We will not, after our experience of Lazarus's history, doubt an instant that He is thoughtful about us. He knows the beginnings of our illness, though He keeps at a distance. He knows when to remain away and when to draw near. He notes down the advances of it, and the stages. He tells truly when His

friend Lazarus is sick and when he sleeps. We
all have experience of this in the narrative before us, and henceforth, so be it! will never com-
plain at the course of His providence. Only, we
will beg of Him an increase of faith; — a more
lively perception of the curse under which the
world lies, and of our own personal demerits, a
more understanding view of the mystery of the
Cross, a more devout and implicit reliance on
the virtue of it, and a more confident persuasion that He will never put upon us more than
we can bear, never afflict His brethren with any
woe except for their own highest benefit.

"Tears of Christ at the Grave of Lazarus,"
Parochial and Plain Sermons, p. 567.

39. Why is the thought of the dead a great consola-
tion for us?

On the other hand, while the thought of the dead
is thus a restraint upon us, it is also a great consolation, especially in this age of the world, when
the Universal Church has fallen into errors and
is divided branch against branch. What shall
sustain our faith (under God's grace) when we
try to adhere to the Ancient Truth, and seem
solitary? What shall nerve the "watchman on the
walls of Jerusalem," against the scorn and jealousy of the world, the charge of singularity, of
fancifulness, of extravagance, of rashness? What
shall keep us calm and peaceful within, when

accused of "troubling Israel," and "prophesy-
ing evil"? What but the vision of all Saints of all
ages, whose steps we follow? What but the image of Christ mystically stamped upon our
hearts and memories? The early times of purity
and truth have not passed away! They are
present still! We are not solitary though we seem
so. Few now alive may understand or sanction
us; but those multitudes in the primitive time,
who believed, and, in their past deeds and their
present voices, cry from the Altar. They animate
us by their example; they cheer us by their company; they are on our right hand and our left,
Martyrs, Confessors, and the like, high and low,
who used the same Creeds, and celebrated the
same Mysteries, and preached the same Gospel
as we do. And to them were joined, as ages went
on, even in fallen times, nay, even now in times
of division, fresh and fresh witnesses from the
Church below. In the world of spirits there is no
difference of parties. It is our plain duty indeed
here, to contend even for the details of the Truth
according to our light; and surely there is a Truth
in spite of the discordance of opinions. But that
Truth is at length simply discerned by the spirits of the just; human additions, human institu-
tions, human enactments, enter not with them
into the unseen state. They are put off with the
flesh. Greece and Rome, England and France,
give no colour to those souls which have been
cleansed in the One Baptism, nourished by the

One Body, and moulded upon the One Faith.
Adversaries agree together directly they are
dead, if they have lived and walked in the Holy
Ghost. The harmonies combine and fill the
temple, while discords and imperfections die
away. Therefore is it good to throw ourselves
into the unseen world, it is "good to be there,"
and to build tabernacles for those who speak "a
pure language" and "serve the Lord with one
consent"; not indeed to draw them forth from
their secure dwelling-places, not superstitiously
to honour them, or willfully to rely on them, lest
they be a snare to us, but silently to contemplate
them for our edification; thereby encouraging
our faith, enlivening our patience, sheltering us
from thoughts about ourselves, keeping us from
resting on ourselves, and making us seem to
ourselves (what really we ought ever to be) only
followers of the doctrine of those who have gone
before us, not teachers of novelties, not founders
of schools.

> "The Intermediate State," *Parochial and Plain
> Sermons*, pp. 720-721.

40. *Why does a true Christian view death as a happy event?*

But further (if it be allowable to speculate), one
can even conceive the same kind of feeling, and
a most transporting one, to come over the soul
of the faithful Christian, when just separated

from the body, and conscious that his trial is once for all over. Though his life has been a long and painful discipline, yet when it is over, we may suppose him to feel at the moment the same sort of surprise at its being ended as generally follows any exertion in this life, when the object is gained and the anticipation over. When we have wound up our minds for any point of time, any great event, an interview with strangers, or the sight of some wonder, or the occasion of some unusual trial, when it comes, and is gone, we have a strange reverse of feeling from our changed circumstances. Such, but without any mixture of pain, without any lassitude, dullness, or disappointment, may be the happy contemplation of the disembodied spirit; as if it said to itself, "So all is now over; this is what I have so long waited for; for which I have nerved myself; against which I have prepared, fasted, prayed, and wrought righteousness. Death is come and gone — it is over. Ah! is it possible? What an easy trial, what a cheap price for eternal glory! A few sharp sicknesses, or some acute pain awhile, or some few and evil years, or some struggles of mind, dreary desolateness for a season, fightings and fears, afflicting bereavements, or the scorn and ill-usage of the world — how they fretted me, how much I thought of them, yet how little really they are! How contemptible a thing is human life, contemptible in itself, yet in its effects invaluable! for it has been to me like a small seed of easy purchase, germinating and ripening into bliss everlasting."

"The Greatness and Littleness of Human Life,"*Parochial and Plain Sermons*, p. 865.

41. *What can we do to insure that God will know us at the end of our lives?*

You have one work only, to bear your cross after Him. Resolve in His strength to do so. Resolve to be no longer beguiled by "shadows of religion," by words, or by disputings, or by notions, or by high professions, or by excuses, or by the world's promises or threats. Pray Him to give you what Scripture calls "an honest and good heart," or "a perfect heart," and, without waiting begin at once to obey Him with the best heart you have. Any obedience is better than none, any profession which is disjoined from obedience, is a mere pretense and deceit. Any religion which does not bring you nearer to God is of the world. You have to seek His face; obedience is the only way of seeking Him. All your duties are obediences. If you are to believe the truths He has revealed, to regulate yourselves by His precepts, to be frequent in His ordinances, to adhere to His Church and people, why is it, except because *He* has bid you? and to do what He bids is to obey Him, and to obey Him is to approach Him. Every act of obedience is an approach — an approach to Him who is not far off, though He seems so, but close behind this material framework; earth and sky are but a veil going between Him and us; the day will come when He will rend that veil, and show Himself to us. And then, according as we have waited for Him, will He recompense us. If we have forgotten him, He will not know us; but "blessed are those servants whom the Lord, when He cometh, shall find watching... He shall gird Himself, and make them sit down to eat, and will come forth and serve them. And if He shall come in the second watch, or come in the third watch, and find them so, blessed are those servants." *Luke* xii. 37, 38. May this be the portion of every one of us! It is hard to attain it; but it is woeful to fail. Life is short; death is certain; and the world to come is everlasting.

"Watching," *Parochial and Plain Sermons*, p. 938.

42. *Why is death a comfort to the servant of God?*

Yes, so it is; the world contrives to forget that men have souls, it looks upon them all as mere parts of some great visible system. This continues to move on; to this the world ascribes a sort of life and personality. When one or another of its members die, it considers them only as falling out of the system, and as come to naught. For a minute, perhaps, it thinks of them in sorrow, then leaves them — leaves them for ever. It keeps its eye on things seen and temporal.

Truly whenever a man dies, rich or poor, an immortal soul passes to judgment; but somehow we read of the deaths of persons we have seen or heard of, and this reflection never comes across us. Thus does the world really cast off men's souls, and recognizing only their bodies, it makes it appear as if "that which befalleth the sons of men befalleth beasts, even one thing befalleth them, as the one dieth so dieth the other; yea, they have all one breath, so that a man hath no preeminence over a beast, for all is vanity." *Eccles.* iii. 19.

But let us follow the course of a soul thus casting off the world, and cast off by it. It goes forth as a stranger on a journey. Man seems to die and to be no more, when he is but quitting us, and is really beginning to live. Then he sees sights which before it did not even enter into his mind to conceive, and the world is even less to him than he to the world. Just now he was lying on the bed of sickness, but in that moment of death what an awful change has come over him! What a crisis for him! There is stillness in the room that lately held him; nothing is doing there, for he is gone, he now belongs to others, he now belongs entirely to the Lord who bought him; to Him he returns; but whether to be lodged safely in His place of hope, or to be imprisoned against the great Day, that is another matter, that depends on the deeds done in the body, whether good or evil. And now what are his thoughts?

How infinitely important now appears the value
of time, now when it is nothing to him! Nothing; for though he spend centuries waiting for
Christ, he cannot now alter his state from bad to
good, or from good to bad. What he dieth that
he must be for ever; as the tree falleth so must it
lie. This is the comfort of the true servant of God,
and the misery of the transgressor.

"The Lapse of Time," *Parochial and Plain
Sermons*, pp. 1411-1412.

· VI ·

Heaven

43. Who live in the invisible world?

But all this does not interfere with the existence of that other world which I speak of, acting upon us, yet not impressing us with the consciousness that it does so. It may as really be present and exert an influence as that which reveals itself to us. And that such a world there is, Scripture tells us. Do you ask what it is, and what it contains? I will not say that all that belongs to it is vastly more important than what we see, for among things visible are our fellow men, and nothing created is more precious and noble than a son of man. But still, taking the things which we see altogether, and the things we do not see altogether, the world we do not see is on the whole a much higher world than that which we do see. For, first of all, He is there Who is above all beings, Who has created all before Whom they all are as nothing, and with Whom nothing can be compared. Almighty God, we know exists more really and absolutely than any of those fellow men whose existence is conveyed to us through the senses; yet we see Him not, hear Him not, we do but "feel after Him," yet without finding Him. It appears, then, that the things which are seen are but a part, and but a secondary part of the beings about us, were it only on this ground, that Almighty God, the Being of beings, is not in their number but among "the things which are not seen." Once, and once only, for thirty-three years, has He condescended to become one of the beings which are seen, when He, the Second Person of the Ever-blessed Trinity, was, by an unspeakable mercy, born of the Virgin Mary into this sensible world. And then He was seen, heard, handled; He ate, He drank, He slept, He conversed, He went about, He acted as other men: but excepting this brief period, His presence has never been perceptible; He has never made us conscious of His existence by means of our senses. He came, and He retired beyond the veil: and to us individually, it is as if He had never shown Himself; we have all little sensible experience of His presence. Yet "He liveth ever more."

And in that other world are the souls also of the dead. They too, when they depart hence, do not cease to exist, but they retire from this visible scene of things; or, in other words, they cease to act toward us and before us *through our senses*. They live as they lived before; but that outward frame, through which they were able to hold communion with other men, is in some way, we know not how, separated from them, and dries away and shrivels up as leaves may drop off a tree. They remain, but without the usual means of approach toward us, and correspondence with us. As when a man loses his voice or hand, he still exists as before, but cannot any longer talk or write, or otherwise hold intercourse with us; so when he loses not voice and hand only, but his whole frame, or is said to die, there is nothing to show that he is gone, but we have lost our means of apprehending him.

Again: Angels also are inhabitants of the world invisible, and concerning them much more is told us than concerning the souls of the faithful departed, because the latter "rest from their labours"; but the angels are actively employed among us in the Church. They are said to be "ministering spirits, sent forth to minister for them who shall be heirs of salvation." No Christian is so humble but he has angels to attend on him, if he lives by faith and love. *Heb.* 1.14.

"The Invisible World," *Parochial and Plain Sermons*, pp. 853-854.

· VII ·

Happiness

44. What is the secret of the triumph of Christ's
    Kingdom?

Man is not sufficient for his own happiness; he
is not happy except the Presence of God be with
him. When he was created, God breathed into
him that supernatural life of the Spirit which is
his true happiness: and when he fell, he lost the
divine gift, and with it his happiness also. Ever
since he has been unhappy; ever since he has a
void within him which needs filling, and he
knows not how to fill it. He scarcely realizes his
own need: only his actions show that he feels it,
for he is ever restless when he is not dull and
insensible, seeking in one thing or another that
blessing which he has lost. Multitudes, indeed,
there are, whose minds have never been opened;
and multitudes who stupefy and deaden their
minds, till they lost their natural hunger and
thirst: but, whether aware of their need or not,
whether made restless by it or not, still all men
have it, and the Gospel supplies it; and then,
even if they did not recognize their want by nature, they at length learn it by its supply. This,

then, is the secret of the triumph of Christ's Kingdom. Soldiers of this world receive their bounty-money on enlisting. They take it, and become the servants of an earthly prince: shall not they, much more, be faithful, yea, unto the death, who have received the earnest of the true riches, who have been fed with the hidden manna, who have "tasted the good word of God, and the powers of the world to come," and "the graciousness of the Lord," and "the peace which passeth all understanding"? It is the Presence of Christ which makes us members of Christ: "neither shall they say, Lo here! and Lo there! for the kingdom of God is within us."

"Invisible Presence of Christ," *Sermons on Subjects of the Day*, pp. 312-313.

45. *What are the thoughts that make us rejoice in every day and hour that passes?*

Heaven at present is out of sight, but in due time, as snow melts and discovers what it lay upon, so will this visible creation fade away before those greater splendours which are behind it, and on which at present it depends. In that day shadows will return, and the substance show itself. The sun will grow pale and be lost in the sky, but it will be before the radiance of Him whom it does but image, the Sun of Righteousness, with healing on His wings, who will come forth in visible form, as a bridegroom out of his chamber, while His perishable type decays. The stars which surround it will be replaced by Saints and Angels circling His throne. Above and below, the clouds of the air, the trees of the field, the waters of the great deep will be found impregnated with the forms of everlasting spirits, the servants of God which do His pleasure. And our own mortal bodies will then be found in like manner to contain within them an inner man, which will then receive its due proportions, as the soul's harmonious organ, instead of that gross mass of flesh and blood which sight and touch are sensible of. For this glorious manifestation the whole creation is at present in travail, earnestly desiring that it may be accomplished in its season.

"The Greatness and Littleness of Human Life," *Parochial and Plain Sermons*, p. 867.

46. *Who satisfies completely the desires of the human heart?*

We have most of us by nature longings more or less, and aspirations, after something greater than this world can give. Youth, especially, has a natural love of what is noble and heroic. We like to hear marvellous tales, which throw us out of things as they are, and introduce us to things that are not. We so love the idea of the invisible, that we even build fabrics in the air for ourselves, if heavenly truth be not vouchsafed us. We love to fancy ourselves involved in circumstances of danger or trial, and acquitting ourselves well under them. Or we imagine some perfection, such as earth has not, which we follow, and render it our homage and our heart. Such is the state more or less of young persons before the world alters them, before the world comes upon them, as it often does very soon, with its polluting, withering, debasing, deadening influence, before it breathes on them, and blights and parches, and strips off their green foliage, and leaves them, as dry and wintry trees without sap or sweetness. But in early youth we stand with our leaves and blossoms on, which promise fruit; we stand by the side of the still waters, with our hearts beating high, with longings after our unknown good, and with a sort of contempt for the fashions of the world, with a contempt for the world, even though we engage in it. Even though we allow ourselves in our degree to listen to it, and to take part in its mere gaieties and amusements, yet we feel the while that our happiness is not there; and we have not yet come to think, though we are in the way to think, that all that is beyond this world is after all an idle dream. We are on our way to think it, for no one stands where he was; he desires after what he has not, his earnest thoughts after things unseen, if not fixed on their true objects, catch at something which he does see, something earthly and perishable, and seduce him from God. But I am speaking of men *before* that time, before they have given their hearts to the world, which promises them true good, then cheats them, and then makes them believe that there is no truth anywhere, and that they were fools for thinking it. But before that time, they have desires after things above this world, which they embody in some form of this world, because they have no other way at all of realizing them. If they are in humble life, they dream of becoming their own masters, rising in the world, and securing an independence; if in a higher rank, they have ambitious thoughts of gaining a name and exercising power. While their hearts are thus unsettled, Christ comes to them, if they will receive Him, and promises to satisfy their great need, this hunger and thirst which wearies them. He does not wait till they have learned to ridicule high feelings as mere romantic dreams: He comes to the young; He has them baptized betimes, and then promises them, and in a higher way, those unknown blessings which they yearn after. He seems to say in the words of the Apostle, "What ye ignorantly worship, that declare I unto you." You are seeking what you see not, I give it you; you desire to be great, I will make you so; but observe how — just in the reverse way to what you expect; the way to real glory is to become unknown and despised.

"The Weapons of Saints," *Parochial and Plain Sermons*, pp. 1372-1373.

47. *How may we gain true happiness?*

Seek we great things? We must seek them where they really are to be found, and in the way in which they are to be found; we must seek them as He has set them before us, who came into the world to enable us to gain them. We must be willing to give up present hope for future enjoyment, this world for the unseen. The truth is (though it is difficult for us to admit it heartily), our nature is not at first in a state to enjoy happiness, even if we had it offered to us. We seek for it, and we feel we need it; but (strange though it is to say, still so it is) we are not fitted to be happy. If then at once we rush forward to seek enjoyment, it will be like a child's attempting to walk before his strength is come. If we would gain true bliss we must cease to seek it as an end; we must postpone the prospect of enjoying it. For we are by nature in an unnatural state; we must be changed from what we are when born before we can receive our greatest good. And as in sickness sharp remedies are often used, or irksome treatment, so it is with our souls; we must go through pain, we must practise self-denial, we must curb our wills, and purify our hearts, before we are capable of any lasting solid peace. To attempt to gain happiness, except in this apparently tedious and circuitous way, is a labour lost; it is building on the sand; the foundation will soon give way, though the house looks fair for a time. To be gay and thoughtless, to be self-indulgent and self-willed, is quite out of character with our real state. We must learn to know ourselves, and to have thoughts and feelings becoming ourselves. Impetuous hope and undisciplined mirth ill suit a sinner. Should *he* shrink from low notions of himself, and sharp pain, and mortification of natural wishes, whose guilt called down the Son of God from heaven to die upon the cross for him? May he live in pleasure here, and call this world his home, while he reads in the Gospel of his Saviour's lifelong affliction and disappointment?

"Jeremiah, a Lesson for the Disappointed,"
Parochial and Plain Sermons, p. 1633.

· VIII ·

Sin

48. Why do the greatest saints commit venial sins?

Let a person be ever so good an accountant, he will add up a sum wrongly now and then, though you could not guess beforehand when or why he was to fail. Let him get by heart a number of lines ever so perfectly, and say them accurately over, yet it does not follow that he will say them a dozen times and be accurate throughout. So it is with our religious duties; we may be able to keep from every sin in particular as the particular temptation comes, but this does not hinder its being certain that we shall not in fact keep from all sins, though that "all" is made up of those particular sins. This is how the greatest saints come to commit venial or lesser sins, though grace they have sufficient to keep them from any sin whatever. It is the result of human frailty; nothing could keep the saints from such falls, light as they may be, but a special prerogative, and this, the Church teaches, has been granted to the Blessed Virgin, and apparently to her alone. Now these lesser

or venial sins do not separate the soul from God,
or forfeit its perseverance in grace; and they are
permitted by the Giver of all grace for a good
purpose, to humble us, and to give us an incen-
tive to works of penance.

"Perseverance in Grace," *Discourses
Addressed to Mixed Congregations*, p. 128.

49. *How may pride destroy us?*

Pride infatuates man, and self-indulgence and
luxury work their way unseen — like some
smouldering fire, which for a while leaves the
outward form of things unaltered. At length the
decayed mass cannot hold together, and breaks
by its own weight, or on some slight and accidental external violence. As the Prophet says:
"This iniquity shall be to you as a breach ready
to fall, swelling out (or bulging) in a high wall,
whose breaking cometh *suddenly at an instant*."

"Secrecy and Suddenness of Divine Visitations,"
Parochial and Plain Sermons, p. 297.

50. *Why do seemingly good persons leave the Church?*

I repeat, I am speaking of those whom God sees
to be willful in their separation; and though we
cannot know who are such, and therefore can
pronounce judgment absolutely on no one, yet I
would have all those who are thrown with per-

sons who, being separatists, may be such, to bear
in mind that their seeming to be holy and religious ever so much, does not prove they are really so, supposing they have this one secret sin
chargeable upon them in God's books. Just as a
man may be in good health, may have his arms
and hands his own, his head clear, his mind active, and yet may have one organ diseased, and
the disease not at once appear, but be latent, and
yet be mortal, bringing certain death in the event,
so may it be with them. As, in the instance just
now taken, a man may be upright and noble-
minded, with a single purpose and a high reso-
luteness, kind and gentle, self-denying and
charitable, and yet towards one certain individual may cherish feelings of revenge, and
thereby show that some principle short of the
love of God rules his heart — so may it be with
those who seem to be good men, and willfully
leave the Church. Their religious excellences,
whatever these may be, are of no avail really
against this or any other willful sin.

> "Moral Consequences of Single Sins,"
> *Parochial and Plain Sermons*, pp. 757-758.

51. *Do sins of weakness tend to grievous sins?*

It remains to show that these sins of infirmity
tend to those which are greater, and forfeit grace;
which is not the least important point which
comes under consideration.

An illustration will explain what I mean, and may throw light on the whole subject. You know it continually happens that some indisposition overtakes a man, such that persons skilled in medicine, when asked if it is dangerous, answer, "Not at present, but they do not know what will come of it; it may turn out something very serious; but there is nothing much amiss yet; at the same time, if it be not checked, and, much more, if it be neglected it will be serious." This, I conceive, is the state of Christians day by day, as regards their souls; they are always ailing, always on the point of sickness; they are sickly, easily disarranged, obliged to take care of themselves against air, sun, and weather; they are full of tendencies to all sorts of grievous diseases, and are continually showing these tendencies, in slight symptoms; but they are not yet in a dangerous way. On the other hand, if a Christian falls into any serious sin, then he is at once cast out of grace, as a man who falls into a pestilential fever is quite in a distinct state from one who is merely in delicate health.

Now with respect to this progress of sin from infirmity to transgression, here, as before, we have no need to go to Scripture in proof of a truth which every day teaches us, that men begin with little sins and go on to great sins, that the course of sin is a continuous declivity, with nothing to startle those who walk along it, and that the worst transgressions seem trifles to the sinner, and that the lightest infirmities are grievous to the holy. "He that despiseth small things," says the wise man, "shall fall by little and little"; this surely is the doctrine of inspired Scripture throughout.

"Transgression and Infirmities," *Parochial and Plain Sermons*, pp. 1079-1080.

52. *How may we describe a person who cannot surrender all resentment?*

Another illustration may be drawn from the state of mind which not infrequently is found in a person who has been injured or insulted, and is bound in duty to forgive the offenders. I am supposing a well-meaning and religious man; and he often lies under the temptation to forgive them up to a certain point, but at the same time to make a reserve in favour of his own dignity, or to satisfy his sense of justice, and thus to take the matter in part into his own hands. He cannot get himself honestly to surrender every portion of resentment, and to leave his cause simply to God, as remembering the words, "Vengeance is Mine; I will repay." *Rom.* xii. 19. This reluctance is sometimes seen very clearly under other circumstances, in the instance of children, who, whether they be out of temper, or obstinate, or otherwise what they should not be, cannot bring themselves to do that very thing which they ought to do, which is enough, which comes up to the mark. They are quite conscious that they are wrong, and they wish to be right; and they will do a number of good things short of what is required of them; they will show their wish to be at one again with the parties who are displeased with them; they will go round about their duty — but from pride, or other wrong feeling, they shrink from going close to it, and, as it were, embracing it. And so again, if they have been at fault, they will make excuses, or half confess; they will do much, but they cannot bring themselves to do a whole deed, and make a clean breast of it.

"The Testimony of Conscience," *Parochial and Plain Sermons*, pp. 1105-1106.

53. *Why are sinners unhappy?*

I say, when anyone, man or woman, young or old, is conscious that he or she is going wrong, whether in greater matter or less, whether in not coming to church when there is no good excuse, neglecting private prayer, living carelessly, or indulging in known sin — this bad conscience is from time to time a torment to such persons. For a little while, perhaps, they do not feel it but then the pain comes on again. It is a keen, harassing, disquieting, hateful pain, which hinders sinners from being happy. They may have *pleasures*, but they cannot be *happy*. They know that God is angry with them; and they know that, at some time or other, He will visit, He will judge, He will punish. They try to get this out of their minds, but the arrow sticks fast there; it keeps its hold. They try to laugh it off, or to be bold and daring, or to be angry and violent. They are loud or unkind in their answers to those, who remind them of it either in set words, or by their example. But it keeps its hold. And so it is, that all men who are not very abandoned, bad men as well as good, wish that they were holy as God is holy, pure as Christ was pure, even though they do not try to be, or pray to God to make them, holy and pure; not that they *like* religion, but that they know, they are convinced in their reason, they feel sure, that religion alone is happiness.

"Love of Religion, a New Nature," *Parochial and Plain Sermons*, pp. 1511-1512.

· IX ·

Grace

54. *Did Christ bring a higher nature into this world of human persons?*

These are some of the arguments on which the
world relies in defending the interests of this life
against those of the next. It says that the consti-
tution of our body and the powers of our mind
tend towards an end short of the next life; and
therefore that religion, or the thought of the next
world, is unnatural. I answer by admitting that
religion is in this sense unnatural; but I main-
tain that Christ came to bring in a higher nature
into this world of men, and that this could not
be done except by interfering with the nature
which originally belongs to it. Where the spiritual system runs counter to the natural, the natural must give way. God has graciously willed to
bring us to heaven; to practise a heavenly life
on earth, certainly, is a thing above earth. It is
like trying to execute some high and refined
harmony on an insignificant instrument. In attempting it, that instrument would be taxed beyond its powers, and would be sacrificed to great
ideas beyond itself. And so, in a certain sense,

this life, and our present nature, is sacrificed for heaven and the new creature; that while our outward man perishes, our inward man may be renewed day by day.

> "Faith and the World," *Sermons on Subjects of the Day*, p. 87.

55. *What two attendants accompany Christ's entry into us?*

Because the Brazen Serpent in the wilderness healed by being looked at, they consider that Christ's Sacrifice saves by the mind's contemplating it. This is what they call casting themselves upon Christ — coming before Him simply and without self-trust, and being saved by faith. Surely we ought so to *come* to Christ; surely we must believe; surely we must look; but the question is, in what form and manner He *gives* Himself to us: and it will be found that, when He enters into us, glorious as He is in Himself, pain and self-denial are His attendants. Gazing on the Brazen Serpent did not heal; but God's invisible communication of the gift of health to those who gazed. So also justification is wholly the work of God; it comes from God to us; it is a power exerted on our souls by Him, as the healing of the Israelites was a power exerted on their bodies. The gift must be brought *near* to us; it is not like the Brazen Serpent, a mere external, material, local sign; it is a spiritual gift, and, as being such, admits of being applied to us individually. Christ's Cross does not justify by being looked at, but by being applied; not by as merely beheld by faith, but by being actually set up within us, and that not by our act, but by God's invisible grace. Men sit, and gaze, and speak of the great Atonement, and think this is appropriating it; not more truly than kneeling to the material cross itself is appropriating it. Men say that faith is an apprehending and applying; faith cannot really apply the Atonement; man cannot make the Saviour of the world his own; the Cross must be brought home to us, not in word, but in power, and this is the work of the Spirit. This is justification; but when imparted to the soul, it draws blood, it heals, it purifies, it glorifies.

Lectures on the Doctrine of Justification, pp. 174-175.

56. *Why is Christianity superior to mere human knowledge of morality?*

Christianity raises men from earth, for it comes from heaven; but human morality creeps, struts, or frets upon the earth's level, without wings to rise. The Knowledge School does not contemplate raising man above himself; it merely aims at disposing of his existing powers and tastes, as is most convenient, or is practicable under circumstances. It finds him, like the victims of the French Tyrant, doubled up in a cage in which he can neither lie, stand, sit, nor kneel, and its

highest desire is to find an attitude in which his
unrest may be least.

Discussions and Arguments, pp. 269-270, 272.

57. *Does God alone sanctify us who are free to resist that sanctification?*

Again, "It is God which worketh in you both to
will and to do of His good pleasure." *Phil.* ii. 13.
What is this but a declaration, that on the whole
all our sanctification is from first to last God's
work? how does it interfere with this, to say that
we may effectually resist that work? Might it not
truly be said that the cure of a sick person was
wholly attributable to the physician, without
denying that the former, had he so chosen, might
have obstinately rejected the medicine, or that
there might have been (though there was not)
some malignant habit of body, which completely
baffled the medical art? Does the chance of failure make it less the physician's work when there
is not failure?

"Human Responsibility," *Parochial and Plain
Sermons*, pp. 431-432.

58. *What great truth is the foundation of all true doctrine as to the way of salvation?*

"Without Me ye can do nothing," *John* xv. 5 and
St. Paul, "I can do all things through Christ, that
strengtheneth me." And again, in the Epistle
before us, "Who maketh thee to differ from an-

other? and what hast thou that thou didst not receive? now if thou didst receive it, why dost thou glory, as if thou hadst not received it?" I *Cor*. iv. 7.

This is that great truth which is at the foundation of all true doctrine as to the way of salvation. All teaching about duty and obedience, about attaining heaven, and about the office of Christ towards us, is hollow and insubstantial, which is not built *here*, in the doctrine of our original corruption and helplessness; and, in consequence, of original guilt and sin. Christ Himself indeed is the foundation, but a broken, self-abased, self-renouncing heart is (as it were) the ground and soil in which the foundation must be laid; and it is but building on sand to profess to believe in Christ, yet not to acknowledge that without Him we can do nothing. It is what is called the Pelagian heresy, of which many of us perhaps have heard the name. I am not, indeed, formally stating what that heresy consists in, but I mean, that, speaking popularly, I may call it the belief, that "holy desires, good counsels, and just works," can come of *us*, can be *from* us, as well as *in* us: whereas they are from God only; from whom, and not from ourselves, is that righteousness, sanctification, and redemption, which is in us — from whom is the washing away of our inward guilt, and the implanting in us of a new nature. But when men take it for granted that they are natural objects

of God's favour — when they view their privileges and powers as natural things — when they
look upon their Baptism as an ordinary work,
bringing about its results as a matter of course
— when they come to Church without feeling
that they are highly favoured in being allowed
to come — when they do not understand the necessity of prayer for God's grace — when they
refer everything to system, and subject the pro-
visions of God's free bounty to the laws of cause
and effect — when they think that education will
do everything, and that education is in their own
power — when, in short, they think little of the
Church of God, which is the great channel of
God's mercies, and look upon the Gospel as a
sort of literature or philosophy, contained in
certain documents, which they may use as they
use the instruction of other books; then, not to
mention other instances of the same error, are
they practically Pelagians, for they make themselves their own centre, instead of depending
on Almighty God and His ordinances.

> "Righteousness Not Of Us But In Us,"
> *Parochial and Plain Sermons*, pp. 1036-1037.

59. *Is God the total strength of my soul?*

I say, by birth we are in a state of defect and
want; we have not all that is necessary for the
perfection of our nature. As the body is not complete in itself, but requires the soul to give it a

meaning, so again the soul till God is present with it, and manifested in it, has faculties and affections without a ruling principle, object or purpose. Such it is by birth, and this Scripture signifies to us by many figures; sometimes calling human nature blind, sometimes hungry, sometimes unclothed, and calling the gift of the Spirit light, health, food, warmth, and raiment; all by way of teaching us what our first state is, and what our gratitude should be to Him Who has brought us into a new state. For instance, "Because thou sayest, I am rich, and increased in goods, and have need of nothing; and knowest not that thou art wretched, and miserable, and poor, and blind, and naked: I counsel thee to buy of Me gold tried in the fire, that thou mayest be rich; and white raiment, that thou mayest be clothed… and anoint thine eyes with eye salve, that thou mayest see." Again, "God, who commanded the light to shine out of darkness, hath shined in our hearts, to give the light of the knowledge of the glory of God, in the face of Jesus Christ." Again, "Awake, thou that sleepest, and arise from the dead, and Christ shall give thee light." Again, "whosoever drinketh of the water that I shall give him, shall never thirst; but the water that I shall give him shall be in him a well of water springing up into everlasting life." *Apoc.* iii. 17, 18. II *Cor.* iv. 6. *Eph.* v. 14. *John* iv. 14.

"The Thought of God the Stay of the Soul,"
Parochial and Plain Sermons, pp. 1147-1148.

· X ·

Faith

60. What is true faith?

True faith is what may be called colourless, like air or water; it is but the medium through which the soul sees Christ; and the soul as little really rests upon it and contemplates it, as the eye can see the air. When, then, men are bent on holding it (as it were) in their hands, curiously inspecting, analyzing, and so aiming at it, they are obliged to colour and thicken it, that it may be seen and touched. That is, they substitute for it something or other, a feeling, notion, sentiment, conviction, or act of reason, which they may hang over, and dote upon. They rather aim at experiences (as they are called) within them, than at Him that is without them.

Lectures on the Doctrine of Justification, p. 336.

61. Why do we believe?

Does a child trust his parents because he has proved to himself that they are such, and that they are able and desirous to do him good, or from the instinct of affection? We *believe* because we *love*. How plain a truth! What gain is it to be wise above that which is written? Why, O men, deface with your minute and arbitrary philosophy the simplicity, the reality, the glorious liberty of the inspired teaching? Is this your godly jealousy for Scripture? this your abhorrence of human additions?

It is the doctrine, then, of the text, that those who believe in Christ, believe because they know Him to be the Good Shepherd; and they know Him by His voice; and they know His voice, because they are His sheep; that they do not follow strangers and robbers, because they know not the voice of strangers: moreover, that they know and follow Christ, upon His loving them. "I am come that they might have life... The hireling fleeth, because he is a hireling, and careth not for the sheep." The divinely enlightened mind sees in Christ the very Object whom it desires to love and worship — the Object correlative of its own affections; and it trusts Him, or believes, from loving Him.

"Love the Safeguard of Faith Against Superstition," *Oxford University Sermons*, pp. 235-236.

62. *What was Abraham's distinguishing grace?*

But since time, and circumstances, and their own use of the gift, and their own disposition and character, have much influence on the mode of its manifestation, so it happens that each good man has his own distinguishing grace, apart from the rest, his own particular hue and fragrance and fashion, as a flower may have. As, then, there are numberless flowers on the earth, all of them flowers, and so far like each other; and all springing from the same earth, and nourished by the same air and dew, and none without beauty; and yet some are more beautiful than others; and of those which are beautiful, some excel in colour, and others in sweetness, and others in form; and then, again, those which are sweet have such perfect sweetness, yet so distinct, that we do not know how to compare them together, or to say which is the sweeter: so it is with souls filled and nurtured by God's secret grace. Abraham, for instance, Jacob's forefather, was the pattern of faith. This is insisted on in Scripture, and it is not here necessary to show that he was so. It will be sufficient to say that he left his country at God's word; and, at the same word, took up the knife to slay his own son. Abraham seems to have had something very noble and magnanimous about him. He followed God in the dark as promptly, as firmly, with as cheerful a heart, and bold a stepping, as if he were in broad daylight. There is something very great in this; and, therefore St. Paul calls Abraham *our* father, the father of Christians as well as of Jews. For we are especially bound to walk by faith, not by sight; and are blessed in faith, and justified by faith, as was faithful Abraham.

> "Remembrance of Past Mercies," *Parochial and Plain Sermons*, p. 1000.

63. *How can we come gradually to a real apprehension of the truths of faith?*

At first children do not know that they are responsible beings; but by degrees they not only feel that they are, but reflect on the great truth, and on what it implies. Some persons recollect a time as children when it fell on them to reflect what they were, whence they came, whither they tended, why they lived, what was required of them. The thought fell upon them long after they had heard and spoken of God; but at length they began to realize what they had heard, and they began to muse about themselves. So, too, it is in matters of this world. As our minds open, we gradually understand where we are in human society. We have a notion of ranks and classes, of nations, of countries. We begin to see how we stand relatively to others. Thus a man differs from a boy; he has a general view of things; he sees their bearings on each other; he sees his own position, sees what is becoming, what is expected of him, what his duty is in the community, what his rights. He understands his place in the world, and, in a word, he is at home in it.

Alas, that while we thus grow in knowledge in matters of time and sense, yet we remain children in knowledge of our heavenly privileges! St. Paul says, that whereas Christ is risen, He "hath raised us up together, and made us sit together in heavenly places in Christ Jesus." *Eph.* ii. 6. This is what we have still to learn; to know our place, position, situation as "children of God, members of Christ, and inheritors of the kingdom of heaven." We are risen again, and we know it not. We begin our Catechism by confessing that we are risen, but it takes a long life to apprehend what we confess. We are like people waking from sleep, who cannot collect their thoughts at once, or understand where they are. By little and little the truth breaks upon us. Such are we in the present world; sons of light, gradually waking to a knowledge of themselves. For this let us meditate, let us pray, let us work — gradually to attain to a real apprehension of what we are. Thus, as time goes on, we shall gain first one thing, then another. By little and little we shall give up shadows and find the substance. Waiting on God day by day, we shall make progress day by day, and approach to the true and clear view of what He has made us to be in Christ. Year by year we shall gain something, and each Easter, as it comes, will enable us more to rejoice with heart and understanding in that great salvation which Christ then accomplished.

This we shall find to be one great providential benefit arising from those duties which He exacts of us. Our duties to God and man are not only duties done to Him, but they are means of enlightening our eyes and making our faith apprehensive. Every act of obedience has a tendency to strengthen our convictions about heaven. Every sacrifice makes us more zealous; every self-denial makes us more devoted. This is a use, too, of the observance of sacred seasons; they wean us from this world, they impress upon us the reality of the world which we see not. We trust, if we thus proceed, we shall understand more and more where we are. We humbly trust that, as we cleanse ourselves from this world, our eyes will be enlightened to see the things which are only spiritually discerned. We hope that to us will be fulfilled in due measure the words of the beatitude, "Blessed are the pure in heart, for they shall see God." *Matt.* v. 8. We have good hope, which cannot deceive us, that if we wait upon God, as the saints have ever waited, with fastings and prayers — if we seek Him as Anna sought Him, or St. Peter at Joppa, or holy Daniel before them, Christ will be manifested to us; the day will dawn, and the daystar arise in our hearts. We shall see the sign of the Son of man in heaven; we shall eat of the hidden manna, and possess that secret of the Lord which is with those that fear Him; and, like St. Paul, we shall "know whom we have believed, and be persuaded that He is able to keep that which we have committed unto Him against that day." 2 *Tim* i. 12.

"Difficulty of realizing sacred privileges,"
Parochial and Plain Sermons, pp. 1238-1240.

· XI ·

God's Love for Us

64. Does God love sinners?

"God so loved the world, as to give His only-begotten Son." He loved mankind in their pollution, in spite of the abhorrence with which that pollution filled Him. He loved them with a father's love, who does not cast off a worthless son once for all, but is affectionate toward his person, while he is indignant at his misconduct. He loved them for what still remained in them of their original excellence, which was in its measure a reflection of His own. He loved them before He redeemed them, and He redeemed them because He loved them. This is that "philanthropy" or "humanity" of God our Saviour, of which the inspired writers speak.

"St. Paul's Gift of Sympathy," *Sermons Preached on Various Occasions*, pp. 106-107.

65. How can we know that we are in God's favour?

We indeed have not knowledge such as His; were we ever so high in God's favour, a certainty

of our justification would not belong to us. Yet,
even to know only thus much, that infirmities
are no necessary mark of reprobation, that God's
elect have infirmities, and that our own sins may
possibly be no more than infirmities, this surely,
but itself, is a consolation. And to reflect that at
least God continues us visibly in His Church;
that He does not withdraw from us the ordinances of grace; that He gives us means of instruction, patterns of holiness, religious guidance, good books; that He allows us to frequent
His house, and to present ourselves before Him
in prayer and Holy Communion; that He gives
us opportunities of private prayer; that He has
given us a care for our souls; an anxiety to secure our salvation; a desire to be more strict and
conscientious, more simple in faith, more full of
love than we are; all this will tend to soothe and
encourage us, when the sense of our infirmities
makes us afraid. And if further, God seems to
be making us His instruments for any purpose
of His, for teaching, warning, guiding, or com-
forting others, resisting error, spreading the
knowledge of the truth, or edifying His Church,
this too will create in us the belief, not that God
is certainly pleased with us, for knowledge of
mysteries may be separated from love, but that
He has not utterly forsaken us in spite of our
sins, that He still remembers us, and knows us
by name, and desires our salvation. And further,
if, for all our infirmities, we can point to some

occasions on which we have sacrificed anything for God's service, or to any habit of sin or evil tendency of nature which we have more or less overcome, or to any habitual self-denial which we practice, or to any work which we have accomplished to God's honour and glory; this perchance may fill us with the humble hope that God is working in us, and therefore is at peace with us. And, lastly, if we have, through God's mercy, an inward sense of our own sincerity and integrity, if we feel that we can appeal to God with St. Peter, that we love Him only, and desire to please Him in all things — in proportion as we feel this, or at such times as we feel it, we have an assurance shed abroad on our hearts, that we are at present in His favour, and are in training for the inheritance of His eternal kingdom.

"Sins of Infirmity," *Parochial and Plain Sermons*, pp. 1089-1090.

· XII ·

Our Love for God

66. Is love the seed of holiness?

Love, then, is the seed of holiness, and grows into all excellences, not indeed destroying their peculiarities, but making them what they are. A weed has stalk, leaves, and flowers; so has a sweet-smelling plant; because the latter is sweet-smelling, it does not cease to have stalk, leaves, and flowers; but they are all pleasant, because they come of it. In like manner, the soul which is quickened with the spirit of love has faith and hope, and a number of faculties and habits, some of which it might have without love, and some not; but any how, in that soul one and all exist *in* love, though distinct from it; as stalk, leaves, and flowers are as distinct and entire in one plant as in another, yet vary in their quality, according to the plant's nature.

"Faith and Love," *Parochial and Plain Sermons*, p. 924.

· XIII ·

Love of Neighbor

*67. How should a clergyman correct another
person?*

It is a clergyman's duty to rebuke by virtue of
his office. And then, after all, supposing it be
clearly our duty to manifest our religious profession in this pointed way before another, in
order to do so modestly we must do so kindly
and cheerfully, as gently as we can; doing it as
little as we can help; not making matters worse
than they are, or showing our whole Christian
stature (or what we think to be such), when we
need but put out a hand (so to say) or give a
glance. And above all (as I have already said),
acting as if we thought, nay, really thinking, that
it may be the offender's turn some day to rebuke us; not putting ourselves above him, feeling our great imperfections, and desirous he
should rebuke us, should occasion require it, and
in prospect thanking him; acting, that is, in the
spirit in which you warn a man in walking
against rugged ground, which may cause him a

fall, thinking him bound by your friendly conduct to do the like favour to you.

"Profession Without Ostentation,"
Parochial and Plain Sermons, p. 103.

68. *How did St. Paul practice fraternal charity?*

There are saints in whom grace supersedes nature; so was it not with this great Apostle; in him grace did but sanctify and elevate nature. It left him in the full possession, in the full exercise, of all that was human, which was not sinful. He who had the constant contemplation of his Lord and Saviour, and if he saw Him with his bodily eyes, was nevertheless as susceptible of the affections of human nature and the influences of the external world, as if he were a stranger to that contemplation. Wonderful to say, he who had rest and peace in the love of Christ, was not satisfied without the love of man; he whose supreme reward was the approbation of God, looked out for the approval of his brethren. He who depended solely on the Creator, yet made himself dependent on the creature. Though he had That which was Infinite, he would not dispense with the finite. He loved his brethren, not only "for Jesus' sake," to use his own expression, but for their own sake also. He lived in them; he felt with them and for them; he was anxious about them; he gave them help, and in turn he looked for comfort from them. His mind was like some instrument of music, harp or viol, the strings of which vibrate, though untouched, by the notes which other instruments give forth, and he was ever, according to his own precept, "rejoicing with them that rejoice, and weeping with them that wept"; and thus he was the least magisterial of all teachers, and the gentlest and most amiable of all rulers. "Who is weak," he asks, "and I am not weak? who is scandalized, and I am not on fire?" And, after saying this, he characteristically adds, "If I must needs glory, I will glory of the things that concern my infirmity."

"St. Paul's Gift of Sympathy," *Sermons Preached on Various Occasions*, pp. 113-114.

· XIV ·

Use of Creatures

69. How should a Christian enjoy God's temporal blessings?

And in like manner, as they must not defraud themselves of Christian privileges, neither need they give up God's temporal blessings. All the beauty of nature, the kind influences of the seasons, the gifts of sun and moon, and the fruits of the earth, the advantages of civilized life, and the presence of friends and intimates; all these good things are but one extended and wonderful type of God's benefits in the Gospel. Those who aim at perfection will not reject the gift, but add a corrective; they will add the bitter herbs to the fatted calf, and the music and dancing; they will not refuse the flowers of earth, but they will toil in plucking up the weeds. Or if they refrain from one temporal blessing, it will be to reserve another; for this is one great mercy of God, that while He allows us a discretionary use of His temporal gifts, He allows a discretionary abstinence also; and He almost enjoins upon us the use of some, lest we should forget that this earth is His creation, and not of the evil one. I am not denying that there are certain individuals raised up from time to time to a still more self-denying life, and who have a corresponding measure of divine consolations. As some men are Apostles, others Confessors and Martyrs, as Missionaries in heathen countries may be called to give up all for Christ; so there are doubtless those, living in peaceable times and among their brethren, who acknowledge a call to give up everything whatever for the sake of the Gospel, and in order to be perfect; and to become as homeless and as shelterless, and as resourceless and as solitary, as the holy Baptist in the wilderness; but extraordinary cases are not for our imitation, and it is as great a fault to act without a call as to refuse to act upon one.

"Indulgence in Religious Privileges," *Sermons on Subjects of the Day*, pp. 123-124.

70. *How can wealth keep us from making God the one true object of our affections?*

The most obvious danger which worldly possessions present to our spiritual welfare is, that they become practically a substitute in our hearts of that One Object to which our supreme devotion is due. They are present; God is unseen. They are means at hand of effecting what we want: whether God will hear our petitions for those wants is uncertain; or rather I may say, certain in the negative. Thus they minister to the corrupt inclinations of our nature; they promise and are able to be gods to us, and such gods too as require no services, but, like dumb idols, exalt the worshipper, impressing him with a notion of his own power and security. And in this consist their chief and most subtle mischief. Religious men are able to repress, nay extirpate sinful desires, the lust of the flesh and of the eyes, gluttony, drunkenness, and the like, love of amusements and frivolous pleasures and display, indulgence in luxuries of whatever kind; but as to wealth, they cannot easily rid themselves of a secret feeling that it gives them a footing to stand upon, an importance, a superiority, and in consequence they get attached to this world, lose sight of the duty of bearing the Cross, become dull and dim-sighted, and lose their delicacy and precision of touch, are numbed (so to say) in their fingers' ends, as regards religious interests and prospects. To risk all upon Christ's word seems somehow unnatural to them, extravagant, and evidences a morbid excitement; and death, instead of being a gracious, however awful release, is not a welcome subject of thought. They are content to remain as they are, and do not contemplate a change. They desire and mean to serve God, nay actually do serve Him in their measure; but not with the keen sensibilities, the noble enthusiasm, the grandeur and elevation of soul, the dutifulness and affectionateness towards Christ which become

a Christian, but as Jews might obey, who had
no Image of God given them except this created
world, "eating their bread with joy, and drink-
ing their wine with a merry heart," caring that
"their garments be always white, and their head
lacking no ointment, living joyfully with the wife
whom they love all the days of the life of their
vanity," and "enjoying the good of their labour."
Eccles. ix. 7-9; v. 18. Not, of course, that the due
use of God's temporal blessings is wrong, but
to make them the object of our affections, to allow them to beguile us from the "One Husband"
to whom we are espoused, is to mistake the
Gospel for Judaism.

> "The Danger of Riches," *Parochial and
> Plain Sermons*, pp. 444-445.

71. Why does Sunday worship benefit us?

This, let it be observed, is one important benefit
arising from the institution of the Lord's day.
Over and above the privilege of being allowed
one day in seven for religious festivity, the Christian may accept it as a merciful break-in upon
his usual employments, lest they should engross
him. Most men, indeed, perceive this; they will
feel wearied with the dust of this world when
Saturday comes, and understand it to be a mercy
that they are not obliged to go on toiling without cessation. But still, there are many who, if it
were not an express ordinance of religion, would

feel tempted, or think it their duty, to continue their secular labours, even though the custom of society allowed them to rest. Many, as it is, are so tempted; that is, at times, when they have some pressing object in view, and think they cannot afford to lose a day: and many always — such, for instance, as are in certain professions, which are not regulated (as trade is, more or less) by times and places. And great numbers, it is to be feared, yield to the temptation; and the evil effect of it shows itself in various miserable ways, even in the overthrow of their health and reason. In all these cases, then, the weekly Services of prayer and praise come to us as a gracious relief, a pause from the world, a glimpse of the third heaven, lest the world should rob us of our hope, and enslave us to that hard master who is plotting our eternal destruction.

"Religious Worship, A Remedy for Excitements," *Parochial and Plain Sermons*, p. 692.

72. *How does a saint differ from an ordinary religious man?*

I say in this — that he sets before him as the one object of life, to please and obey God; that he ever aims to submit his will to God's will; that he earnestly follows after holiness; and that he is habitually striving to have a closer resemblance to Christ in all things. He exercises himself, not only in social duties, but in Christian graces; he is not only kind but meek; not only generous, but humble; not only persevering, but patient; not only upright, but forgiving; not only bountiful, but self-denying; not only contented, but meditative and devotional. An ordinary man thinks it enough to do as he is done by; he will think it fair to resent insults, to repay injuries, to show a becoming pride, to insist on his rights, to be jealous of his honour, when in the wrong to refuse to confess it, to seek to be rich, to desire to be well with the world, to fear what his neighbors will say. He seldom thinks of the Day of Judgment, seldom thinks of sins past, says few prayers, cares little for the Church, has no zeal for God's truth, spends his money on himself. Such is an ordinary Christian, and such is not one of God's elect. For the latter is more than just, temperate, and kind; he has a devoted love of God, high faith, holy hope, overflowing charity, a noble self-command, a strict conscientiousness, humility never absent, gentleness in speech, simplicity, modesty, and unaffectedness, an unconsciousness of what his endowments are, and what they make him in God's sight. This is what Christianity has done in the world; such is the result of Christian teaching; viz. to elicit, foster, mature the seeds of heaven which lie hid in the earth, to multiply (if it may be said) images of Christ, which, though they be few, are worth all else that is among men, and are an ample recompense and "a crown of rejoicing"

for Apostles and Evangelists "in the presence of
our Lord Jesus Christ at His coming." I *Thess*. ii.
19.

"The Visible Church for the Sake of the
Elect," *Parochial and Plain Sermons*, p. 825.

73. *Should beginners in the spiritual life mortify themselves according to their strength?*

Who is there, who, on setting out on a journey,
sees before him his destination? How often,
when a person is making for a place which he
has never seen, he says to himself, that he cannot believe that at a certain time he really will
be there? There is nothing in what he at present
sees, which conveys to him the assurance of the
future; and yet, in time, that future will be
present. So it is as regards our spiritual course:
we know not what we shall be; but begin it, and,
at length, by God's grace, you will end it; not,
indeed, with the grace He now has given, but
by fresh and fresh grace, fuller and fuller, increased according to your need. Thus you will
end, if you do but begin; but begin not *with* the
end; begin with the beginning; mount up the
heavenly ladder step by step. Fasting is a duty;
but we ought to fast according to our strength.
God requires nothing of us beyond our strength;
but the utmost according to our strength. "She
has done what she could," was his word of com-
mendation to Mary. Now, to forget or to miss

this truth, is very common with beginners, even through mere ignorance or inadvertence. They know not what they can do, and what they cannot, as not having yet tried themselves. And then, when what they hoped was easy, proves a great deal too much for them, they fail, and then are dispirited. They wound their conscience, as being unable to fulfill their own resolves, and they are reduced to a kind of despair; or they are tempted to be reckless, and to give up all endeavours whatever to obey God, because they are not strong enough for everything. And thus it often happens, that men rush from one extreme to another; and even profess themselves free to live without any rule of self-government at all, after having professed great strictness, or even extravagance, in their mode of living.

"Apostolic Abstinence: A Pattern for Christians," *Parochial and Plain Sermons*, pp. 1197-1198.

· XV ·

Our Purpose in Life

74. What is the purpose of life?

St. Paul on one occasion speaks of the world as a scene in a theater. Consider what is meant by this. You know actors on a stage are on an equality with each other really, but for the occasion they assume a difference of character; some are high, some are low, some are merry, and some sad. Well, would it not be a simple absurdity in any actor to pride himself on his mock diadem, or his edgeless sword, instead of attending to his part? what, if he did but gaze at himself and his dress? what, if he secreted, or turned to his own use, what was valuable in it? Is it not his business, and nothing else, to act his part well? Common sense tells us so. Now we are all actors in this world; we are one and all equal, we shall be judged as equals as soon as life is over; yet, equal and similar in ourselves, each has his special part at present, each has his work, each has his mission — not to indulge his passions, not to make money, not to get a name in the world, not to save himself trouble, not to follow his bent, not to be selfish and self-willed, but to do what God puts on him to do.

"God's Will: The End of Life," *Discourses Addressed to Mixed Congregations*, p. 112.

75. *What is the simple view of our purpose in life?*

Oh that we could take that simple view of things, as to feel that the one thing which lies before us is to please God! What gain is it to please the world, to please the great, nay, even to please those whom we love, compared with this? What gain is it to be applauded, admired, courted, followed, compared with this one aim, of not being disobedient to a heavenly vision? What can this world offer comparable with that insight into spiritual things, that keen faith, that heavenly peace, that high sanctity, that everlasting righteousness, that hope of glory, which they have who in sincerity love and follow our Lord Jesus Christ?

Let us beg and pray Him day by day to reveal Himself to our souls more fully; to quicken our senses; to give us sight and hearing, taste and touch of the world to come; so to work within us that we may sincerely say, "Thou shalt guide me with Thy counsel, and after that receive me in glory. Whom have I in heaven but Thee? and there is none upon earth that I desire in comparison of Thee: my flesh and my heart faileth; but God is the strength of my heart, and my portion for ever." *Ps.* 72:24-26.

"Divine Calls," *Parochial and Plain Sermons,*
p. 1574.

· XVI ·

Peace

76. *Why does a true Christian remain calm at all times?*

Did you ever look at an expanse of water and observe the ripples on the surface? Do you think that disturbance penetrates below it? Nay; you have seen or heard of fearful tempests on the sea; scenes of horror and distress, which are in no respect a fit type of an Apostle's tears or sighings about his flock. Yet even these violent commotions do not reach into the depths. The foundations of the ocean, the vast realms of water which girdle the earth, are as tranquil and as silent in the storm as in a calm. So is it with the souls of holy men. They have a well of peace springing up within them unfathomable; and though the accidents of the hour may make them seem agitated, yet in their hearts they are not so. Even angels joy over sinners repentant, and, as we may therefore suppose, grieve over sinners impenitent, yet who shall say that they have not perfect peace? Even Almighty God Himself deigns to speak of His being grieved, and angry, and rejoicing — yet is He not the Unchangeable? And in like manner, to compare human with divine, St. Paul had perfect peace, as being stayed in soul on God, though the trials of life might vex him.

For, as I have said, the Christian has a deep, silent, hidden peace which the world sees not — like some well in a retired and shady place, difficult of access. He is the greater part of his time by himself, and when he is in solitude, that is his real state. What he is when left to himself and to his God, that is his true life. He can bear himself; he can (as it were) joy in himself, for it is the grace of God within him, it is the presence of the Eternal Comforter, in which he joys. He can bear, he finds it pleasant, to be with himself at all times — "never less alone than when alone." He can lay his head on his pillow at night, and own in God's sight, with overflowing heart, that he wants nothing — that he "is full and abounds" — that God has been all things to him, and that nothing is not his which God could give him. More thankfulness, more holiness, more of heaven he needs indeed, but the thought that he can have more is not a thought of trouble, but of joy. It does not interfere with his peace to know that he may grow nearer God. Such is the Christian's peace, when, with a single heart and the Cross in his eye, he addresses and commends himself to Him with whom the night is as clear as the day. St. Paul says that "the peace of God shall *keep* our hearts and minds." By "keep" is

meant "guard," or "garrison," our hearts; so as
to keep out enemies. And he says, our "hearts
and minds" in contrast to what the world sees
of us. Many hard things may be said of the Christian, and done against him, but he has a secret
preservative or charm, and minds them not.

"Equanimity," *Parochial and Plain Sermons*,
pp. 994-995.

77. *How can I acquire peace of soul?*

And, it may be, this is something of the Apostle's
meaning, when he speaks of the witness of the
Spirit. Perhaps he is speaking of that satisfaction and rest which the soul experiences in proportion as it is able to surrender itself wholly to
God, and to have no desire, no aim, but to please
Him. When we are awake, we are conscious we
are awake, in a sense in which we cannot fancy
we are when we are asleep. When we have discovered the solution of some difficult problem
in science, we have a conviction about it which
is distinct from that which accompanies fancied
discoveries or guesses. When we realize a truth
we have a feeling which they have not, who take
words for things. And so, in like manner, if we
are allowed to find that real and most sacred
Object on Which our heart may fix itself, a fullness of peace will follow, which nothing but it
can give. In proportion as we have given up the
love of the world, and are dead to the creature,

and, on the other hand, are born of the Spirit
unto love of our Maker and Lord, this love carries with it its own evidence whence it comes.
Hence the Apostle says, "The Spirit itself beareth
witness with our spirit, that we are the children
of God." Again, he speaks of Him "Who hath
sealed us, and given the earnest of the Spirit in
our hearts." *Rom.* viii. 16. II *Cor.* i. 22.

"The Thought of God the Stay of the Soul,"
Parochial and Plain Sermons, p. 1152.

· XVII ·
Prayer

78. How can we bring ourselves into the direct presence of God?

When men begin all their works with the thought of God, acting for His sake, and to fulfill His will, when they ask His blessing on themselves and their life, pray to Him for the objects they desire, and see Him in the event, whether it be according to their prayers or not, they will find everything that happens tends to confirm them in the truths about Him which live in their imagination, varied and unearthly as those truths may be. Then they are brought into His presence as that of a Living Person, and are able to hold converse with Him, and that with a directness and simplicity, with a confidence and intimacy, *mutatis mutandis*, which we use towards an earthly superior; so that it is doubtful whether we realize the company of our fellow-men with greater keenness than these favoured minds are able to contemplate and adore the Unseen, Incomprehensible Creator.

Grammar of Assent, pp. 106-107.

79. *How should we address God in prayer?*

This will be seen more clearly, by considering how differently we feel towards and speak of our friends as present or absent. Their presence is a check upon us; it acts as an external law, compelling us to do or not do what we should not do or do otherwise, or should do but for it. This is just what most men lack in their religion at present — such an external restraint arising from the consciousness of God's presence. Consider, I say, how differently we speak of a friend, however intimate, when present or absent; consider how we feel, should it so happen that we have begun to speak of him as if he were not present, on finding suddenly that he is; and that, though we are conscious of nothing but what is loving and open towards him. There is a tone of voice and a manner of speaking about persons absent, which we should consider disrespectful, or at least inconsiderate, if they were present. When that is the case, we are ever thinking more or less, even though unconsciously to ourselves, how they will take what we say, how it will affect them, what they will say to us or think of us in turn. When a person is absent, we are tempted perhaps confidently to say what his opinion is on certain points — but should he be present, we qualify our words; we hardly like to speak at all, from the vivid consciousness that we may be wrong, and that he is present to tell us so. We are very cautious of pronouncing what his feel-

ings are on the matter at hand, or how he is dis-
posed towards ourselves; and in all things we
observe a deference and delicacy in our conduct
towards him. Now, if we feel this towards our
fellows, what shall we feel in the presence of the
All-knowing, All-searching Judge of men? What
is respect and consideration in the case of our
fellows, becomes godly fear as regards Almighty
God; and they who do not fear Him, in one word,
do not believe that He sees and hears them. If
they did, they would cease to boast so confidently of His favourable thoughts of them, to
foretell His dealings, to pronounce upon His rev-
elations, to make free with His Name, and to address Him familiarly.

> "Reverence, a Belief in God's Presence,"
> *Parochial and Plain Sermons*, pp. 965-966.

80. What is meditating on Christ?

It is simply this, thinking habitually and con-
stantly of Him and of His deeds and sufferings.
It is to have Him before our minds as One whom
we may contemplate, worship, and address
when we rise up, when we lie down, when we
eat and drink, when we are at home or abroad,
when we are working, or walking, or at rest,
when we are alone, and again when we are in
company; this is meditating. And by this, and
nothing short of this, will our hearts come to feel
as they ought. We have stony hearts, hearts as

hard as the highways; the history of Christ makes no impression on them. And yet, if we would be saved, we must have tender, sensitive, living hearts, our hearts must be broken, must be broken up like ground, and dug, and watered, and tended, and cultivated, till they become as gardens, gardens of Eden, acceptable to our God, gardens in which the Lord God may walk and dwell; filled, not with briars and thorns, but with all sweet-smelling and useful plants, with heavenly trees and flowers. The dry and barren waste must burst forth into springs of living water. This change must take place in our hearts if we would be saved; in a word, we must have what we have not by nature, faith and love; and how is this to be effected, under God's grace, but by godly and practical meditation through the day?

St. Peter describes what I mean, when he says, speaking of Christ, "Whom having not seen ye love: in whom, though now ye see Him not, yet believing, ye rejoice with joy unspeakable and full of glory." 1 *Pet.* i. 8.

Christ is gone away; He is not seen; we never saw Him, we only read and hear of Him. It is an old saying, "Out of sight, out of mind." Be sure, so it *will* be, so it *must* be with us, as regards our blessed Saviour, unless we make continual efforts all through the day to think of Him, His love, His precepts, His gifts, and His promises. We must recall to mind what we read in the Gospels and in holy books about Him; we must bring before us what we have heard in church; we must pray God to enable us to do so, to bless the doing so, and to make us do so in a simpleminded, sincere, and reverential spirit. In a word, we must meditate, for all this is meditation; and this even the most unlearned person can do, and will do, if he has a will to do it.

Now of such meditation, or thinking over Christ's deeds and sufferings, I will say two things; the first of which would be too plain to mention, except that, did I not mention it, I might seem to forget it, whereas I grant it. It is this: that such meditation is not at all pleasant at first. I know it; people will find it at first very irksome, and their minds will gladly slip away to other subjects. True: but consider, if Christ thought your salvation worth the great sacrifice of voluntary sufferings for you, should not you think (what is your own concern) your own salvation worth the slight sacrifice of learning to meditate upon those sufferings? Can a less thing be asked of you, than, when He has done the work, that you should only have to believe in it and accept it.

And my second remark is this: that it is only by slow degrees that meditation is able to soften our hard hearts, and that the history of Christ's trials and sorrows really moves us. It is not only once thinking of Christ or twice thinking of Christ that will do it. It is by going on quietly and steadily, with the thoughts of Him in our mind's eye, that by little and little we shall gain something of warmth, light, life, and love. We shall not perceive ourselves changing. It will be like the unfolding of the leaves in spring. You do not see them grow; you cannot, by watching, detect it. But every day, as it passes, has done something for them; and you are able, perhaps, every morning to say that they are more advanced than yesterday. So it is with our souls; not indeed every morning, but at certain periods, we are able to see that we are more alive and religious than we were, though during the interval we were not conscious that we were advancing.

"Christ's Privations: A Meditation for Christians," *Parochial and Plain Sermons,* pp. 1202-1204.

· XVIII ·

Christ

81. Who is Christ?

When Christ, the great Prophet, the great
Preacher, the great Missionary, came into the
world, He came in a way the most holy, the most
august, the most glorious. Though He came in
humiliation, though He came to suffer, though
He was born in a stable, though He was laid in a
manger, yet He issued from the womb of an
Immaculate Mother, and His infant form shone
with heavenly light. Sanctity marked every lin-
eament of His character and every circumstance
of His mission. Gabriel announced His incarnation; a Virgin conceived, a Virgin bore, a Virgin
suckled Him; His foster father was the pure and
saintly Joseph; angels proclaimed His birth; a
luminous star spread the news among the hea-
thens; the austere Baptist went before His face;
and a crowd of shriven penitents, clad in white
garments and radiant with grace, followed Him
wherever He went. As the sun in heaven shines
through the clouds, and is reflected in the land-
scape, so the eternal Sun of justice, when He rose

upon the earth, turned night into day, and in His brightness made all things bright.

"Men, not Angels, the Priests of the Gospel," *Discourses Addressed to Mixed Congregations*, pp. 43-44.

82. *How does the world reflect God's glory?*

Such is the world; but Christ came to make a new world. He came into the world to regenerate it in Himself, to make a new beginning, to be the beginning of the creation of God, to gather together in one, and recapitulate all things in Himself. The rays of His glory were scattered through the world; one state of life had some of them, another others. The world was like some fair mirror, broken in pieces, and giving back no one uniform image of its Maker. But He came to combine what was dissipated, to recast what was shattered in Himself. He began all excellence, and of His fullness have all we received. When He came, a Child was born, a Son given, and yet He was Wonderful, Counselor, the Mighty God, the Everlasting Father, the Prince of Peace. Angels heralded a Saviour, a Christ, a Lord; but withal, He was "born in Bethlehem," and was "lying in a manger." Eastern sages brought Him gold, for that He was a King, frankincense as to a God; but on the other hand myrrh also, in token of a coming death and burial. At the last, He "bore witness to the truth" before

Pilate as a Prophet, suffered on the cross as our
Priest, while He was also "Jesus of Nazareth, the
King of the Jews."

> "The Three Offices of Christ," *Sermons on*
> *Subjects of the Day*, p. 61.

83. *How did Christ's office towards His disciples differ from that of the Holy Spirit's office?*

But, though our Lord and Saviour sent His Holy
Spirit to be with us on His going away, still there
was a difference between the Spirit's office, and
that which He Himself graciously fulfilled towards His disciples in the days of His flesh; for
their wants were not the same as before. Christ,
while He was with them, had no occasion to
console them under affliction, to stand by them
in trial as their Paraclete; for trial and affliction
did not visit them while He was with them; but,
on the other hand, the Holy Spirit especially
came to give them joy in tribulation. Again, He
came to teach them fully, what our Lord had but
in part revealed; and hence, too, it followed that
the consolation which the Spirit vouchsafed dif-
fered from that which they had received from
Christ, just as the encouragements and rewards
bestowed upon children are far other than those
which soothe and stimulate grown men in ar-
duous duties. And there were, moreover, other
circumstances, much to be dwelt upon, which
altered the state of the Apostles' feelings and

ideas, after their Lord had died and risen again,
and which made them need a consolation different from that which His bodily presence gave
them. There is no reason for supposing that,
while He was with them, they apprehended the
awful truth, that He is very God in our nature.
"I am among you," He said, "as He that serveth."
But on His resurrection He revealed the mystery. St. Thomas adored Him in the words, "My
Lord and my God"; and He forthwith withdrew
Himself from them, not living in their sight as
heretofore, and soon ascending into heaven. It
is plain, that, after such a revelation, the Apostles
could not have returned to their easy converse
with Him, even had He offered it. What had
been, could not be again; their state of childhood,
before "their eyes were opened and they knew
Him." Of necessity then, since they could not
endure to see God and live, did He "vanish out
of their sight." And if, according to His promise, He was to come to them again, it must be
after a new manner, and with a higher consolation.

> "Christian Nobleness," *Sermons on Subjects
> of the Day*, pp. 138-139.

84. *Will silently bearing the Cross increase my
love for Christ?*

Think of the Cross when you rise and when you
lie down, when you go out and when you come

in, when you eat and when you walk and when you converse, when you buy and when you sell, when you labour and when you rest, consecrating and sealing all your doings with this one mental action, the thought of the Crucified. Do not talk of it to others; be silent, like the penitent woman who showed her love in deep subdued acts. She "stood at His feet behind Him weeping, and began to wash His feet with tears, and did wipe them with the hairs of her head, and kissed His feet, and anointed them with the Ointment." And Christ said of her, "Her sins, which are many, are forgiven her, for she loved much; but to whom little is forgiven, the same loveth little." *Luke* 7. 38, 47.

> "Love, the One Thing Needful," *Parochial and Plain Sermons*, p. 1163.

85. *Does the doctrine of the Cross answer the riddle of life?*

The doctrine of the Cross does but teach, though infinitely more forcibly, still after all it does but teach the very same lesson which this world teaches to those who live long in it, who have much experience in it, who know it. The world is sweet to the lips, but bitter to the taste. It pleases at first, but not at last. It looks gay on the outside, but evil and misery lie concealed within. When a man has passed a certain number of years in it, he cries out with the Preacher,

"Vanity of vanities, all is vanity." Nay, if he has not religion for his guide, he will be forced to go further, and say, "All is vanity and vexation of spirit"; all is disappointment; all is sorrow; all is pain. The sore judgments of God upon sin are concealed within it, and force a man to grieve whether he will or no. Therefore the doctrine of the Cross of Christ does but anticipate for us our experience of the world. It is true, it bids us grieve for our sins in the midst of all that smiles and glitters around us; but if we will not heed it, we shall at length be forced to grieve for them from undergoing their fearful punishment.

"The Cross of Christ the Measure of the World,"
Parochial and Plain Sermons, pp. 1231-1232.

86. *Why is the doctrine of the Cross of Christ the heart of religion?*

This being the case, the great and awful doctrine of the Cross of Christ, which we now commemorate, may fitly be called, in the language of figure, the *heart* of religion. The heart may be considered as the seat of life; it is the principle of motion, heat, and activity; from it the blood goes to and fro to the extreme parts of the body. It sustains the man in his powers and faculties; it enables the brain to think; and when it is touched, man dies. And in like manner the sacred doctrine of Christ's Atoning Sacrifice is the vital principle on which the Christian lives, and without which Christianity is not. Without it no other doctrine is held profitably; to believe in Christ's divinity, or in His manhood, or in the Holy Trinity, or in a judgment to come, or in the resurrection of the dead, is an untrue belief, not Christian faith, unless we receive also the doctrine of Christ's sacrifice. On the other hand, to receive it presupposes the reception of other high truths of the Gospel besides; it involves the belief in Christ's true divinity, in His true incarnation, and in man's sinful state by nature; and it prepares the way to belief in the sacred Eucharistic feast, in which He who was once crucified is ever given to our souls and bodies, verily and indeed, in His Body and in His Blood. But again, the heart is hidden from view; it is carefully and securely guarded; it is not like the eye set in the forehead, commanding all, and seen of all: and so in like manner the sacred doctrine of the Atoning Sacrifice is not one to be talked of, but to be lived upon; not to be put forth irreverently but to be adored secretly; not to be used as a necessary instrument in the conversion of the ungodly, or for the satisfaction of reasoners of this world, but to be unfolded to the docile and obedient, to young children, whom the world has not corrupted; to the sorrowful, who need comfort, to the sincere and earnest, who need a rule of life; to the innocent, who need warning; and to the established, who have earned the knowledge of it.

"The Cross of Christ the Measure of the World," *Parochial and Plain Sermons*, p. 1233.

· XIX ·

Church

87. What is the great difference between Christianity and heathen belief?

Now, independent of all other considerations, the great difference, in a practical light, between the object of Christianity and of heathen belief, is this — that glory, science, knowledge and whatever other fine names we use, never healed a wounded heart, nor changed a sinful one; but the Divine Word is with power. The ideas which Christianity brings before us are in themselves full of influence, and they are attended with a supernatural gift over and above themselves, in order to meet the special exigencies of our nature. Knowledge is not "power," nor is glory "the first and only fair"; but "Grace," or the "Word," by whichever name we call it, has been from the first a quickening, renovating, organizing principle. It has new created the individual, and transferred and knit him into a social body, composed of members each similarly created. It has cleansed man of his moral diseases, raised him to hope and energy, given him to propagate a brotherhood among his fellows, and to

found a family or rather a kingdom of saints all
over the earth; — it introduced a new force into
the world, and the impulse which it gave continues in its original vigour down to this day.
Each one of us has lit his lamp from his
neighbour, or received it from his fathers, and
the lights thus transmitted are at this time as
strong and clear as if 1800 years had not passed
since the kindling of the sacred flame. What has
glory or knowledge been able to do like this?
Can it raise the dead? can it create a polity? can
it do more than testify man's need and typify
God's remedy?

"The Tamworth Reading Room" (Letter 3),
Discussions and Arguments.

88. How does the Catholic Church value the salvation of one single soul?

The Church aims, not at making a show, but at
doing a work. She regards this world, and all
that is in it, as a mere shadow, as dust and ashes,
compared with the value of one single soul. She
holds that, unless she can, in her own way, do
good to souls, it is no use her doing anything;
she holds that it were better for sun and moon
to drop from heaven, for the earth to fail, and
for all the many millions who are upon it to die
of starvation in extremest agony, so far as temporal affliction goes, than that one soul, I will
not say, should be lost, but should commit one

single venial sin, should tell one willful untruth, though it harmed no one, or steal one poor far-thing without excuse. She considers the action of this world and the action of the soul simply incommensurate, viewed in their respective spheres; she would rather save the soul of one single wild bandit of Calabria, or whining beggar of Palermo, than draw a hundred lines of railroad through the length and breadth of Italy, or carry out a sanitary reform, in its fullest details, in every city of Sicily, except so far as these great national works tended to some spiritual good beyond them.

Difficulties of Anglicans, Vol. I, pp. 239-240.

89. Is the Catholic Church the true Church?

There is but one form of Christianity, my Brethren, possessed of that real internal unity which is the primary condition of independence. Whether you look to Russia, England, or Germany, this note of divinity is wanting. In this country, especially, there is nothing broader than class religions; the established form itself is but the religion of a class. There is one persuasion for the rich, and another for the poor; men are born in this or that sect; the enthusiastic go here, and the sober-minded and rational go there. They make money, and rise in the world, and then they profess to belong to the establishment. This body lives in the world's smile, that in its frown; the one would perish of cold in the world's winter, and the other would melt away in summer. Not one of them undertakes human nature: none compasses the whole man; none places all men on a level; none addresses the intellect and the heart, fear and love, the active and the contemplative. It is considered, and justly, as an evidence of Christianity, that the ablest men have been Christians; not that all sagacious or profound minds have taken up its profession, but that it gained victories among them, such and so many, as to show that it is not the mere fact of ability or learning which is the reason why all are not converted. Such, too, is the characteristic of Catholicity; not the highest in rank, not the meanest, not the most refined, not the rudest, is beyond the influence of the Church; she includes specimens of every class among her children. She is the solace of the forlorn, the chastener of the prosperous, and the guide of the wayward. She keeps a mother's eye for the innocent, bears with a heavy hand upon the wanton, and has a voice of majesty for the proud. She opens the mind of the ignorant, and she prostrates the intellect of even the most gifted. These are not words; she has done it, she does it still, she undertakes to do it. All she asks is an open field, and freedom to act. She asks no patronage from the civil power: in former times and places she indeed has asked it; and, as Protestantism also, has availed herself of the civil sword. It is true she did so, because in certain ages it has been the acknowledged mode of acting, the most expeditious, and open at the time to no objection, and because, where she has done so, the people clamored for it and did it in advance of her; but her history shows that she needed it not, for she has extended and flourished without it. She is ready for any service which occurs; she will take the world as it comes; nothing but force can repress her. See, my Brethren, what she is doing in this country now; for three centuries the civil power has trodden down the goodly plant of grace, and kept its foot upon it; at length circumstances have removed that tyranny, and lo! the fair form of the Ancient Church rises up at once, as fresh and as vigorous as if she had never intermitted her growth. She is the same as she was three centuries ago, ere the present religions of the country existed; you know her to be the same; it is the charge brought against her that she does not change; time and place affect her not, because she has her source where there is neither place nor time, because she comes from the throne of the Illimitable, Eternal God.

"Prospects of the Catholic Missioner," *Discourses Addressed to Mixed Congregations*, pp. 252-254.

90. Has Roman Catholicism linearly descended from primitive Christianity?

On the whole, all parties will agree that, of all existing systems, the present communion of Rome is the nearest approximation in fact to the Church of the Fathers, possible though some may think it, to be nearer still to that Church on paper. Did St. Athanasius or St. Ambrose come suddenly to life, it cannot be doubted what communion he would take to be his own. All surely will agree that these Fathers, with whatever opinions of their own, whatever protests, if we will, would find themselves more at home with such men as St. Bernard or St. Ignatius Loyola, or with the lonely priest in his lodging, or the holy sisterhood of mercy, or the unlettered crowd before the altar, than with the teachers or with the members of any other creed. And may we not add, that were those same Saints, who once sojourned, one in exile, one on embassy, at Treves, to come more northward still, and to travel until they reached another fair city, seated among groves, green meadows, and calm streams, the holy brothers would turn from many a high aisle and solemn cloister which they found there, and ask the way to some small chapel where Mass was said in the populous alley or forlorn suburb?

An Essay on the Development of Christian Doctrine, pp. 113-114.

91. *What historical phenomenon testifies that God established the Catholic Church?*

Dismissing then the thought of the feeble and despised preachers, who went to and fro, let us see what really happened, in the midst of a great Empire, such as the world had never seen, powerful and crafty beyond all former empires, more extensive, and better organized, suddenly a new Kingdom arose. Suddenly in every part of this well-cemented Empire, in the East and West, North and South, as if by some general understanding, yet without any sufficient system of correspondence or centre of influence, ten thousand orderly societies, professing one and the same doctrine, and disciplined upon the same polity, sprang up as from the earth. It seemed as though the fountains of the great deep were broken up, and some new forms of creation were thrown forward from below, the manifold ridges of some "great Mountain," crossing, splitting, disarranging the existing system of things, levelling the hills, filling up the valleys — irresistible as being sudden, unforeseen, and unprovided for — till it "filled the whole earth." *Isa*. xli. 15, 16. This was indeed a "new thing"; and independent of all reference to prophecy, is unprecedented in the history of the world before or since, and calculated to excite the deepest interest and amazement in any really philosophical mind. Throughout the kingdoms and provinces of Rome, while all things looked as usual, the sun rising and setting, the seasons continuing, men's passions swaying them as from the beginning, their thoughts set on their worldly business, on their gain or their pleasures, on their ambitious prospects and quarrels, warrior measuring his strength with warrior, politicians plotting, and kings banqueting, suddenly this portent came as a snare upon the whole earth. Suddenly, men found themselves encompassed with foes, as a camp surprised by night. And the nature of this hostile host was still more strange (if possible) than the coming of it. It was not a foreigner who invaded them, not a barbarian from the north, nor a rising of slaves, nor an armament of pirates, but the enemy rose up from among themselves. The first-born in every house, "from the first-born of Pharaoh on the throne, to the first-born of the captive in the dungeon," unaccountably found himself enlisted in the ranks of this new power, and estranged from his natural friends. Their brother, the son of their mother, the wife of their bosom, the friend that was as their own soul, these were the sworn soldiers of the "mighty army," that "covered the face of the whole earth."

Next, when they began to interrogate this enemy of Roman greatness, they found no vague profession among them, no varying account of themselves, no irregular and uncertain plan of action or conduct. They were all members of strictly and similarly organized societies. Every one in his own district was the subject of a new state, of which there was one visible head, and officers under him. These small kingdoms were indefinitely multiplied, each of them the fellow of the other. Wherever the Roman Emperor travelled, there he found these seeming rivals of his power, the Bishops of the Church. Further, they one and all refused to obey his orders, and the prescriptive laws of Rome, so far as religion was concerned. The authority of the Pagan Religion, which in the minds of Romans was identified with the history of their greatness, was plainly set at nought by these upstart monarchies. At the same time they professed and observed a singular patience and subjection to the civil powers. They did not stir hand or foot in self-defence; they submitted to die, nay, accounted death the greatest privilege that could be inflicted on them. And further, they avowed one and all the same doctrine clearly and boldly; and they professed to receive it from one and the same source. They traced it up through the continuous line of their Bishops to certain twelve or fourteen Jews, who professed to have received it from Heaven. Moreover, they were bound one to another by the closest ties of fellowship; the society of each place to its ruler, and their rulers one with another by an intimate alliance all over the earth. And lastly, in spite of persecution from without, and occasional dissensions from within, they so prospered, that within three centuries

134   NEWMAN FOR EVERYONE

from their first appearance in the Empire, they forced its sovereigns to become members of their confederation; nay, nor ended there, but as the civil power declined in strength, they became its patrons instead of its victims, mediated between it and its barbarian enemies, and after burying it in peace when its hour came, took its place, won over the invaders, subdued their kings, and at length ruled as supreme; ruled, united under one head, in the very scenes of their former suffering, in the territory of the Empire, with Rome itself, the seat of the Imperial government, as a centre. I am not entering into the question of doctrine, any more than of prophecy. I am not inquiring how far this victorious Kingdom was by this time perverted from its original character; but only directing attention to the historical phenomenon. How strange then is the course of the Dispensation! Five centuries compass the rise and fall of other kingdoms; but ten were not enough for the full aggrandizement of this. Its sovereignty was but commencing, when other powers have run their course and are exhausted. And now to this day, that original Dynasty, begun by the Apostles, endures. Through all changes of civil affairs, of race, of language, of opinion, the succession of Rulers then begun, has lasted on, and still represents in every country its original founders. "Instead of its fathers, it has had children, who have been princes in all lands." Truly, this is the vision of a "stone *cut out without hands*," "smiting" the idols of the world, "breaking them in pieces," scattering them "like chaff," and in their place, "filling the whole earth." If there be a Moral Governor over the world, is there not something unearthly in all this, something which we are forced to refer to Him from its marvelousness, something which from its dignity and greatness bespeaks of His hand?

> "The Kingdom of the Saints," *Parochial and Plain Sermons*, pp. 375-377.

92. *What is the outward visible guide to the invisible Church?*

Now, what is that outward visible guide, having the dispensation of what is unseen, but the Christian Ministry, which directs and leads us to the very Holy of Holies, in which Christ dwells by His Spirit? As landmarks or buoys inform the steersman, as the shadow on the dial is an index of the sun's course; so, if we would cross the path of Christ, if we would arrest His eye and engage His attention, if we would interest ourselves in the special virtue and fullness of His grace, we must join ourselves to that Ministry which, when He ascended up on high, He gave us as a relic, and let drop from Him as the mantle of Elijah, the pledge and token of His never-failing grace from age to age. "Tell me, O Thou whom my soul loveth, where Thou feedest, where Thou makest Thy flock to rest at noon; for why should I be as one that turneth aside by the flocks of Thy companions?" *Cant.* i. 7, 8. Such is the petition, as it were, of the soul that seeks for Christ. His answer is as precise as the question. "If thou knowest not, O thou fairest among women, go thy way forth by the *footsteps* of the flock, and feed thy kids beside the *shepherds' tents*." Out of the Church is no salvation; I mean to say out of that great invisible company, who are one and all incorporate in the one mystical body of Christ, and quickened by one Spirit: now, by adhering to the visible Ministry which the Apostles left behind them, we approach unto what we see not, to Mount Zion, to the heavenly Jerusalem, to the spirits of the just, to the first-born elected to salvation, to Angels innumerable, to Jesus the One Mediator, and to God. This heavenly Jerusalem is the true Spouse of Christ and virgin Mother of Saints; and the visible Ministry on earth, the Bishops and Pastors, together with Christians depending on them, at this or that day is *called* the Church, though really but a fragment of it, as being the part of it which is seen and can be pointed out, and as resembling it in type, and witnessing it, and leading towards it. This *invisible* body is the *true* Church, because it changes not, though it is ever increasing. What it has, it keeps and never loses; but what is visible is fleeting and transitory, and continually passes off into the invisible. The visible is ever dying for the increase of the invisible company, and is ever reproduced from out the mass of human corruption, by the virtue of the Spirit lodged in the invisible, and acting upon the world. Generation after generation is born, tried, sifted, strengthened, and perfected. Again and again the Apostles live in their successors, and their successors in turn are gathered unto the Apostles. Such is the efficacy of that inexhaustible grace which Christ has lodged in His Church, as a principle of life and increase, till He comes again. The expiring breath of His Saints is but the quickening of dead souls.

"The Communion of Saints," *Parochial and Plain Sermons*, pp. 834-835.

· XX ·

Mass

93. Why is Jesus our daily Sacrifice?

Our Lord not only offered Himself as a Sacrifice
on the Cross, but He makes Himself a perpetual,
a daily Sacrifice, to the end of time. In the Holy
Mass that One Sacrifice on the Cross once offered is renewed, continued, applied to our benefit. He seems to say, My Cross was raised up
1800 years ago, and only for a few hours — and
very few of my servants were present there —
but I intend to bring millions into my Church.
For their sakes then I will perpetuate my Sacrifice, that each of them may be as though they
had severally been present on Calvary. I will
offer Myself up day by day to the Father, that
every one of my followers may have the oppor-
tunity to offer his petitions to Him, sanctified
and recommended by the all-meritorious virtue
of my Passion. Thus I will be a Priest for ever,
after the order of Melchisedech — My priests
shall stand at the Altar — but not they, but I
rather, will offer. I will not let them offer mere
bread and wine, but I myself will be present
upon the Altar instead, and I will offer up my-

self invisibly, while they perform the outward rite. And thus the Lamb that was slain once for all, though He is ascended on high, ever remains a victim from His miraculous presence in Holy Mass under the figure and appearance of mere earthly and visible symbols.

> "Jesus Our Daily Sacrifice," *Prayers,*
> *Verses, and Devotions,* p. 280.

94. Why is Christ's past death on the Cross ever present?

I look on Thee, the Victim lifted up on Calvary, and I know and protest that that death of Thine was an expiation for the sins of the whole world. I believe and know, that Thou alone couldst have offered a meritorious atonement, for it was Thy Divine Nature which gave Thy sufferings worth. Rather then than I should perish according to my deserts, Thou wast nailed to the Tree and didst die.

Such a sacrifice was not to be forgotten. It was not to be — it could not be — a mere event in the world's history, which was to be done and over, and was to pass away except in its obscure, unrecognized effects. If that great deed was what we believe it to be, what we know it is, it must remain present, though past; it must be a standing fact for all times. Our own careful reflection upon it tells us this; and therefore, when we are told that Thou, O Lord, though Thou hast as-

cended to glory, hast renewed and perpetuated
Thy sacrifice to the end of all things, not only is
the news most touching and joyful, as testifying
to so tender a Lord and Saviour, but it carries
with it the full assent and sympathy of our reason. Though we neither could, nor would have
dared, anticipate so wonderful a doctrine, yet
we adore its very suitableness to Thy perfections,
as well as its infinite compassionateness for us,
now that we are told of it. Yes, my Lord, though
Thou hast left the world, Thou art daily offered
up in the Mass: and, though Thou canst not suffer pain and death, Thou dost still subject Thyself to indignity and restraint to carry out to the
full Thy mercies towards us. Thou dost humble
Thyself daily; for, being infinite, Thou couldst
not end Thy humiliation while they existed for
whom Thou didst submit to it. So Thou
remainest a Priest for ever.

"The Mass," *Prayers, Verses, and Devotions,*
pp. 421-422.

95. *Is it difficult to believe the doctrine of*
   Transubstantiation?

People say that the doctrine of Transubstantiation is difficult to believe; I did not believe the
doctrine till I was a Catholic. I had no difficulty
in believing it, as soon as I believed that the
Catholic Roman Church was the oracle of God,
and that she had declared this doctrine to be part

of the original revelation. It is difficult, impossible, to imagine, I grant; — but how is it difficult to believe? Yet Macaulay thought it so difficult to believe, that he had need of a believer in it of talents as eminent as Sir Thomas More, before he could bring himself to conceive that the Catholics of an enlightened age could resist "the overwhelming force of the argument against it." "Sir Thomas More," he says, "is one of the choice specimens of wisdom and virtue; and the doctrine of transubstantiation is a kind of proof charge. A faith which stands that test, will stand any test." But for myself, I cannot indeed prove it, I cannot tell *how* it is; but I say, "Why should it not be? What's to hinder it? What do I know of substance or matter? just as much as the greatest philosophers, and that is nothing at all;" — so much is this the case, that there is a rising school of philosophy now, which considers phenomena to constitute the whole of our knowledge in physics The Catholic doctrine leaves phenomena alone. It does not say that the phenomena go; on the contrary, it says that they remain; nor does it say that the same phenomena are in several places at once. It deals with what no one on earth knows anything about, the material substances themselves. And, in like manner, of that majestic Article of the Anglican as well as of the Catholic Creed, — the doctrine of the Trinity in Unity. What do I know of the Essence of the Divine Being? I know that my ab-

stract idea of three is simply incompatible with
my idea of one; but when I come to the question
of concrete fact, I have no means of proving that
there is not a sense in which one and three can
equally be predicated of the Incommunicable
God.

Apologia Pro Vita Sua, pp. 239-240.

· XXI ·
Mary

96. *Does Marian doctrine remain constant while Marian devotion changes?*

The sun in the springtime will have to shine many days before he is able to melt the frost, open the soil, and bring out the leaves; yet he shines out from the first notwithstanding, though he makes his power felt but gradually. It is one and the same sun, though his influence day by day becomes greater; and so in the Catholic Church it is the one Virgin Mother, one and the same from first to last, and Catholics may have ever acknowledged her; and yet, in spite of that acknowledgment, their devotion to her may be scanty in one time and place, and overflowing in another.

*Certain Difficulties Felt by Anglicans in
Catholic Teaching,* Vol. II, p. 28.

97. *Why should we accord Mary special honour?*

That subject had saved the king's life, and what was to be done to him in return? The king asked, "What should be done to the man whom the

King desireth to honour?" And he received the
following answer, "The man whom the king
wisheth to honour ought to be clad in the king's
apparel, and to be mounted on the king's saddle,
and to receive the royal diadem on his head; and
let the first among the king's princes and presi-
dents hold his horse, and let him walk through
the streets of the city, and say, 'Thus shall he be
honoured, whom the king hath a mind to
honour.'" So stands the case with Mary; she gave
birth to the Creator, and what recompense shall
be made her? what shall be done to her, who
had this relationship to the Most High? what
shall be the fit accompaniment of one whom the
Almighty has deigned to make, not His servant,
not His friend, not His intimate, but His superior, the source of His second being, the nurse
of His helpless infancy, the teacher of His open-
ing years? I answer, as the king was answered:
Nothing is too high for her to whom God owes
His human life; no exuberance of grace, no ex-
cess of glory, but is becoming, but is to be expected there, where God has lodged Himself,
whence God has issued. Let her "be clad in the
king's apparel," that is, let the fullness of the
Godhead so flow into her that she may be a
figure of the incommunicable sanctity, and
beauty, and glory, of God Himself: that she may
be the Mirror of Justice, the Mystical Rose, the
Tower of Ivory, the House of Gold, the Morning Star. Let her "receive the king's diadem upon

her head," as the Queen of heaven, the Mother
of all the living, the Health of the weak, the Ref-
uge of sinners, the Comforter of the afflicted.
And "let the first amongst the king's princes
walk before her," let angels and prophets, and
apostles, and martyrs, and all saints, kiss the hem
of her garment and rejoice under the shadow of
her throne.

> "On the Fitness of the Glories of Mary,"
> *Discourses Addressed to Mixed Congregations,*
> pp. 362-363.

98. *Why is Mary called the Tower of David?*

A tower in its simplest idea is a fabric for de-
fense against enemies. David, King of Israel,
built for this purpose a notable tower; and as he
is the figure or type of our Lord, so is his tower
a figure denoting our Lord's Virgin Mother.

She is called the Tower of David because
she had so signally fulfilled the office of defending her Divine Son from the assaults of His foes.
It is customary with those who are not Catholics to fancy that the honours we pay to her interfere with the supreme worship which we pay
to Him; that in Catholic teaching she eclipses
Him. But this is the very reverse of the truth.

For if Mary's glory is so very great, how
cannot His be greater still who is the Lord and
God of Mary? He is infinitely above His Mother;
and all that grace which filled her is but the

overflowings and superfluities of His incomprehensible Sanctity. And history teaches us the
same lesson. Look at the Protestant countries
which threw off all devotion to her three centuries ago, under the notion that to put her from
their thoughts would be exalting the praises of
her Son. Has that consequence really followed
from their profane conduct towards her? Just the
reverse — the countries, Germany, Switzerland,
England, which so acted, have in great measure
ceased to worship Him, and have given up their
belief in His Divinity; while the Catholic Church,
wherever she is to be found, adores Christ as
true God and true Man, as firmly as ever she
did; and strange indeed would it be, if it ever
happened otherwise. Thus Mary is the "Tower
of David."

> "Mary is the 'Turris Davidica,' the Tower
> of David," *Prayers, Verses, and Devotions*,
> pp. 170-171.

99. *Why was Jesus born of a human mother?*

When our Lord came upon earth, He might have
created a fresh body for Himself out of nothing
— or He might have formed a body for Himself
out of the earth, as He formed Adam. But He
preferred to be born, as other men are born, of a
human mother. Why did He do so? He did so to
put honour on all those earthly relations and
connections which are ours by nature; and to

teach us that, though He has begun a new creation, He does not wish us to cast off the old creation, as far as it is not sinful. Hence it is our duty to love and honour our parents, to be affectionate to our brothers, sisters, friends, husbands, wives, not only not less, but even more, than it was man's duty before our Lord came on earth. As we become better Christians, more consistent and zealous servants of Jesus, we shall become only more and more anxious for the good of all around us — our kindred, our friends, our acquaintances, our neighbours, our superiors, our inferiors, our masters, our employers. And this we shall do from the recollection how our Lord loved His Mother. He loves her still in heaven with a special love. He refuses her nothing. We then on earth must feel a tender solicitude for all our relations, all our friends, all whom we know or have dealings with. And moreover, we must love not only those who love us, but those who hate us or injure us, that we may imitate Him, who not only was loving to His Mother, but even suffered Judas, the traitor, to kiss Him, and prayed for His murderers on the cross.

"Jesus Son of Mary," *Prayers, Verses, and Devotions*, p. 278.

· XXII ·

Second Coming of Christ

100. How will the Second Coming of Christ occur?

Let these be your thoughts, my Brethren, especially in the spring season, when the whole face of nature is so rich and beautiful. Once only in the year, yet once, does the world which we see show forth its hidden powers, and in a manner manifest itself. Then the leaves come out, and the blossoms on the fruit trees and flowers; and the grass and corn spring up. There is a sudden rush and burst outwardly of that hidden life which God has lodged in the material world. Well, that shows you, as by a sample, what it can do at God's command, when He gives the word. This earth, which now buds forth in leaves and blossoms, will one day burst forth into a new world of light and glory, in which we shall see saints and angels dwelling. Who would think, except from his experience of former springs all through his life, who would conceive two or three months before, that it was possible that the face of nature, which then seemed so lifeless, should become so splendid and varied? How different is a tree, how different is a prospect when leaves are on it and off it! How unlikely it would seem, before the event, that the dry and naked branches should suddenly be clothed with what is so bright and so refreshing! Yet in God's good time leaves come on the trees. The season may delay, but come it will at last. So it is with the coming of that Eternal Spring, for which all Christians are waiting. Come it will, though it delay; yet though it tarry, let us wait for it, "because it will surely come, it will not tarry." Therefore we say day by day, "Thy kingdom come," which means — O Lord, show Thyself; manifest Thyself; Thou that sittest between the cherubim, show Thyself; stir up Thy strength and come and help us. The earth that we see does not satisfy us; it is but a beginning; it is but a promise of something beyond it; even when it is gayest, with all its blossoms on, and shows most touchingly what lies hid in it, yet it is not enough. We know much more lies hid in it than we see. A world of saints and angels, a glorious world, the palace of God, the mountain of the Lord of Hosts, the heavenly Jerusalem, the throne of God and Christ — all these wonders, ever-lasting, all-precious, mysterious, and incomprehensible, lie hid in what we see. What we see is the outward shell of an eternal kingdom; and on that kingdom we fix the eyes of our faith. Shine forth, O Lord, as when on Thy Nativity Thine angels visited the shepherds; let Thy glory blossom forth as bloom and foliage on the trees; change with Thy mighty power this visible world into that diviner world, which as yet we see not; destroy what we see, that it may pass and be transformed into what we believe. Bright as is the sun, and the sky, and the clouds; green as are the leaves and the fields; sweet as is the singing of the birds; we know that they are not all, and we will not take up with a part for the whole. They proceed from the center of love and goodness which is God Himself; but they are not His fullness; they speak of heaven, but are not heaven; they are but as stray beams and dim reflections of His Image; they are but crumbs from the table. We are looking for the coming of the day of God, when all this outward world, fair though it be, shall perish; when the heavens shall be burnt, and the earth melt away. We can bear the loss, for we know it will be but the removing of a veil. We know that to remove the world which is seen, will be the manifestation of the world which is not seen. We know that what we see is a screen hiding from us God and Christ, and His saints and angels. And we earnestly desire and pray for the dissolution of all that we see, from our longing after that which we do not see.

"The Invisible World," *Parochial and Plain Sermons*, pp. 857-859.

101. How may we watch for Christ?

Do you know the feeling in matters of this life, of expecting a friend, expecting him to come, and he delays? Do you know what it is to be in unpleasant company, and to wish for the time to pass away, and the hour strike when you may be at liberty? Do you know what it is to be in anxiety lest something should happen which may happen or may not, or to be in suspense about some important event, which makes your heart beat when you are reminded of it, and of which you think the first thing in the morning? Do you know what it is to have a friend in a distant country, to expect news of him, and to wonder from day to day what he is now doing, and whether he is well? Do you know what it is so to live upon a person who is present with You, that your eyes follow his, that you read his soul, that you see all its changes in his countenance, that you anticipate his wishes, that you smile in his smile, and are sad in his sadness, and are downcast when he is vexed, and rejoice in his successes? To watch for Christ is a feeling such as all these; as far as feelings of this world are fit to shadow out those of another.

He watches *for* Christ, who has a sensitive, eager, apprehensive mind; who is awake, alive, quick-sighted, zealous in seeking and honouring Him; who looks out for Him in all that happens, and who would not be surprised, who would not be over-agitated or overwhelmed, if he found that He was coming at once.

And he watches *with* Christ, who, while he looks on to the future, looks back on the past, and does not so contemplate what his Saviour has purchased for him, as to forget what He has suffered for him. He watches with Christ, who ever commemorates and renews in his own person Christ's Cross and Agony, and gladly takes up that mantle of affliction which Christ wore here, and left behind Him when He ascended. And hence in the Epistles, often as the inspired writers show their desire for His Second Coming, as often do they show their memory of His first, and never lose sight of His Crucifixion in His Resurrection.

"Watching," *Parochial and Plain Sermons*, pp. 932-933.

Notes

3. tents of Cedar (Kedar): Psalm 120:5.
   slime of Babylon: Genesis 11:3.
4. He was in the world: John 1:10.
7. a Pope… a great conqueror: Pius VII and Napoleon Bonaparte.
8. at no time: Acts 14:17.
   in every nation: Acts 10:35.
10. Eusebius (263-339) wrote an important *Ecclesiastical History*.
12. lying wonders: 2 Thessalonians 2:9.
    angel of light: 2 Corinthians 11:14.
    the second beast: Revelation 13:11.
13. Vanity of vanities: Ecclesiastes 1:2.
17. *North and South*: a novel by Elizabeth Gaskell (1855).
29. Pompey's Pillar: a red granite column in Alexandria, erected in 302 A.D.
30. In Roman legend, Tarpeia betrayed Rome to the Sabines. As an ironic reward for her treachery, the Sabines threw their shields on Tarpeia and crushed her to death.
35. Mr. Brown: an imaginary person, presented by Newman as an example of "what a student ought *not* to be."
37. the divine handwriting upon the wall: Daniel 5.
38. Lazarus: John 11.
39. watchman on the walls of Jerusalem: Ezekiel 3:17, 33:7.
    troubling Israel: 1 Kings 18:17.
    prophesying evil: 1 Kings 22:8.
46. What ye ignorantly worship: Acts 17:23.
49. This iniquity shall be: Isaiah 30:13.
55. the Brazen Serpent: Numbers 21.
56. the French Tyrant: Louis XI (1461-1483).
61. the Good Shepherd: John 10.
63. Anna: Luke 2:36-38.
    St. Peter at Joppa: Acts 10.
64. God so loved the world: John 3:16.
68. rejoicing with them: Romans 12:15.
    who is weak: 2 Corinthians 11:29.
    If I must needs glory: 2 Corinthians 11:30.

73. She has done what she could: Mark 14:8.
76. the peace of God: Philippians 4:7.
83. I am among you: Luke 22:27.
    My Lord and my God: John 20:28.
    their eyes were opened: Luke 24:31.
85. Vanity of vanities: Ecclesiastes 1:2.
91. from the first-born of Pharaoh: Exodus 12:29.
    covered the face of the earth: Numbers 22:5, 11.
    Instead of its fathers: Psalm 45:16.
    stone cut out without hands: Daniel 2:34-35.
92. the mantle of Elijah: 2 Kings 2.
93. a Priest forever: Psalm 110:4, Hebrews 5:6.
95. Thomas Babington Macaulay (1800-1859), noted English
    historian and essayist. The quotation is from his essay
    "Ranke's History of the Popes."
97. What should be done: Esther 6:6-9.
98. a notable tower: Song of Songs 4:4.